MARY JOYCE

TAKU TO FAIRBANKS, 1,000 MILES BY DOGTEAM

BY MARY ANNE GREINER

Bloomington, IN  Milton Keynes, UK

AuthorHouse™
1663 Liberty Drive, Suite 200
Bloomington, IN 47403
www.authorhouse.com
Phone: 1-800-839-8640

AuthorHouse™ UK Ltd.
500 Avebury Boulevard
Central Milton Keynes, MK9 2BE
www.authorhouse.co.uk
Phone: 08001974150

© *2007 Mary Anne Greiner. All rights reserved.*

No part of this book may be reproduced, stored in a retrieval system, or transmitted by any means without the written permission of the author.

First published by AuthorHouse 4/13/2007

ISBN: 978-1-4259-8824-1 (sc)

Printed in the United States of America
Bloomington, Indiana

This book is printed on acid-free paper.

ACKNOWLEDGEMENTS

I've had this book on Mary Joyce in the back of my mind for 30 years, since her death in 1976. Recently my enthusiasm was renewed. I had several political cards from the 1950's when Mary ran for Territorial Representative to the Alaskan Legislature, and I'd put one on e-Bay. The person winning it, I discovered, was Ellen Carlee, the curator of the Juneau-Douglas Museum. We exchanged some e-mails and it inspired all of this...my probable one last trip to Juneau, to share Mary's legacy with my daughter Kate, and her husband Aaron Murray. It culminated in my finally taking action on distributing Mary Joyce's materials...to the State of Alaska Library Archives and Juneau museum. The State Archives staff held a tea for us to meet all the people involved in working on the Mary Joyce Collection and helped me realize the extent of interest in Mary's activities.

My thanks to owner Michelle Ward and the entire staff at the remote Taku Lodge who serve up to five outstanding salmon bakes every summer day... Michelle brought us up by float plane, housed us in Killisnoo, the oldest cabin at the lodge, built by Hack Smith in the 30s, and renewed my excitement and awe of Alaska's majesty and the brave and inspiring exploits of Mary Joyce. This is where Mary started her 1,000 mile dogteam trek to Fairbanks...and here is where I decided to finally write the story of this kind and fearless woman.

I discovered a distant cousin last year, Tom Joyce, from Dublin. He is the family historian without a doubt, searching family trees and records all over Ireland and the U.S. He supplied the early Joyce family history for this book, plus scores of wonderful stories and facts.

TABLE OF CONTENTS

ACKNOWLEDGEMENTS v

PART ONE . . . INTRODUCTION 1

PART II . . . THE MANUSCRIPT..21

    1. 1,000 MILES BY DOGTEAM 23

    2. TAKU LODGE TO TULSEQUAH 27

    3. TULSEQUAH TO INKLIN HOUSE 31

    4. INKLIN HOUSE TO ATLIN...35

    5. ATLIN TO WHITEHORSE 41

    6. WHITEHORSE..52

    7. SAFARI BY DOGTEAM WHITEHORSE TO BURWASH LANDING 60

    8. BURWASH LANDING TO SNAG...............................75

    9. SNAG TO TANANA CROSSING 87

    10. FAIRBANKS 105

    11. TANANA CROSSING TO FAIRBANKS 107

    12. FAIRBANKS...AGAIN 118

    13. HOME..123

PART THREE . . . AFTER FAIRBANKS................................127

PHOTOGRAPHS

1. MARY JOYCE, Alaska... xi
2. Mary Joyce's grandparents at Farm in Baraboo, Wisconsin.... 3
3. The Joyce and Daly Families in Reedsburg, Wisconsin. Mary (upper left), her brother Marty (lower right) and father Martin (to Mary's right)... 4
4. Mary Joyce, Graduate, Mercy Nursing School, Chicago. 6
5. Mary Joyce in Hollywood, 1920's. 8
6. Early Taku Lodge, Mary Joyce (standing above dog) with Guests. 11
7. Mary Joyce with Skippy in front of Hole in the Wall Glacier, 1930's... 14
8. Getting Mail on the Taku River... 15
9. Wintering Over at Taku Lodge (Xmas Card, 1930's) 16
10. Mary Serving Supper to Skip and Bug Kitchen of Taku Lodge. 17
11. Guests Inside Taku Lodge with Mary Joyce. 18
12. Leigh Hackley (Hack) Smith on Basement Stair Stoop of Taku Lodge. 19
13. Mary Joyce and Dogteam Leaving for Fairbanks December 22. 1935... 21
14. Mary Joyce in her Trail Gear 70
15. Wanted Dead or Alive Telegram 71
16. Mary and guests in boat on Taku River across from Hole in the Wall Glacier 74
17. Site of Fairbanks Ice Carnival Beauty Contest, 1936.......... 104

18. Mary Joyce and her Dogteam on Richardson Highway, Fairbanks......... 117
19. Fairbanks Airport...Mary Joyce with Joe Crosson............ 122
20. Mary Joyce, Stewardess, with her Parka and Home Grown Mink Coat........ 134
21. Movie Ad for "Orphans of the North" Starring Mary Joyce, circa 1941......... 135
22. Mary at her Quonset Home in Juneau during the WWII years......... 136
23. Fr. Hubbard Saved From Rock by Mary Joyce.......... 137
24. Homestead Cabin of Mary Joyce Up River from Taku Lodge......... 138
25. Mary Joyce at the Top Hat Bar in Juneau.......... 145

MAPS

ROUTE TAKEN BY MARY JOYCE ON HER 1,000 MILE DOGTEAM TRIP FROM TAKU LODGE TO FAIRBANKS, 1935-36......... 48-49

MARY JOYCE, Alaska

PART ONE . . . INTRODUCTION

I'm thrilled to share with you the story of Mary Joyce, transplanted Alaskan, musher, homesteader, hunting lodge owner, mink farmer, pilot, nurse, stewardess, territorial government candidate, beauty pageant entrant, river barge cook, movie actress, bar owner, entrepreneur...and more.

She was my mother's first cousin, and as a youngster in Milwaukee in the 50's I well remember her visits...wearing expensive suits and hats from the 1920's, with remnants of dog hair from her beloved sled dogs. I first visited her in 1962 when Mary operated the Top Hat Bar in Juneau, then moved there in 1969 and rented an apartment from her in the Ferry Way Rooms which were torn down around '72 to widen the alley off South Franklin to a through- street. She had the first-floor space, but no one I know of ever stepped foot inside. The building had been formerly owned by a madam in the heart of an earlier red light district, and Mary charged me half the going rate, plus tax. She was remarkably generous to everyone, but had a thrifty streak, derived from her pioneer days in Alaska when supplies were served up by barge, dogsled, or jerryrigging... nothing was ever wasted. I saw her take unused lemon wedges off restaurant plates "to use at the bah". She had a slight east coast accent, dropping "r's" at the end of words. It didn't come from the mid-west, and it wasn't affected at all, so maybe she just liked it that way. I was sitting next to her on the sofa when she died peacefully at her good friends John and Eileen McKelvey's house in Juneau in 1976 after a short illness. Such a lady...I can't remember ever seeing her really mad. I'll let her tell you about her most famous exploit in her own words....

About a thousand mile dogsled trip from the remote Taku Lodge, 35 miles from Juneau, to Fairbanks where she was the Miss Juneau entrant in the 1936 Miss Alaska contest.

I'll fill in the years before and after, and introduce you to the cast of characters.

MARY JOYCE

Mary Joyce was born in Winfield Township near Baraboo, Wisconsin. She hedged on her age from early on in newspaper articles and drivers license, so I'll honor that, knowing you'll probably notice some age inconsistencies. When she died in Juneau, I asked that her tombstone indicate ARRIVED IN ALASKA 1929 - DIED 1976.

Her grandparents, Patrick and Mary Byrne Joyce married in Karrokeel, County Mayo, Ireland in 1854 and emigrated to Wisconsin 9 years later where they eventually purchased a farm. Mary's father and mother, Martin and Mary Conway Joyce, were living in the small farmhouse when her mother shot and killed herself in the early 1900's when she was only 24. I suspect the Conways didn't much like their daughter's husband as they requested an inquest...and self-inflicted wound was the finding. Mary was partially raised by her aunt and uncle (my grandparents), Dr. Frank and Anna Joyce Daly in nearby Reedsburg, Wisconsin. She grew up known as "Toppy" with siblings Marty Jr. (brother), and 5 Daly cousins, Francis, Jane, Zita, Mary Agnes and Patrick. And she always had an adventurous streak and loved fine clothes and things.

After Mary's senior year in high school in Milwaukee, she completed her schooling at Mercy Hospital Nursing School in Chicago with a registered nursing degree. In photos of the day, Mary was meticulously dressed in latest styles and hats. Around this time there are several pictures of Mary at a church in a wedding dress with train and flower girl and wedding party. I never heard of a marriage from Mary or the family, but a failed or annulled marriage of the day may not have been discussed at the time. Or maybe they were acting parts...I couldn't find a license issued in Chicago and Mary was living at the Nursing School, and single, according to the census that year.

Mary Joyce's grandparents at
Farm in Baraboo, Wisconsin.

The Joyce and Daly Families in Reedsburg, Wisconsin.
Mary (upper left), her brother Marty (lower right)
and father Martin (to Mary's right)

HEADING WEST...

With degree in hand, Mary and friends took a motor trip west, approximating the byways of the intriguing Route 66 ...sightseeing, dude ranching, welcoming the unusual. The destination was Hollywood...the glamour and adventure called and Mary answered by taking a job in the First Aid Station at Paramount Studios, later being promoted to Technical Director for films involving hospital scenes. Her movie "career" began with a bit part in a movie... "Sorrel and Son" in 1926, a film that was re-worked and re-released in 1934. It was up for an academy award. There are glamorous photos taken around this time such as an over the shoulder shot putting on lipstick in a mirror. She had a Chrysler roadster and loved speed, earning a half dozen tickets in a two month period. She wore Caron's Bellodgia perfume, a romantic scent reminiscent of fresh carnations and roses.

She also was a Special Duty Nurse at Hollywood Hospital which is where she met Mrs. Erie Smith and Hack in 1926 and her life was to drastically change.

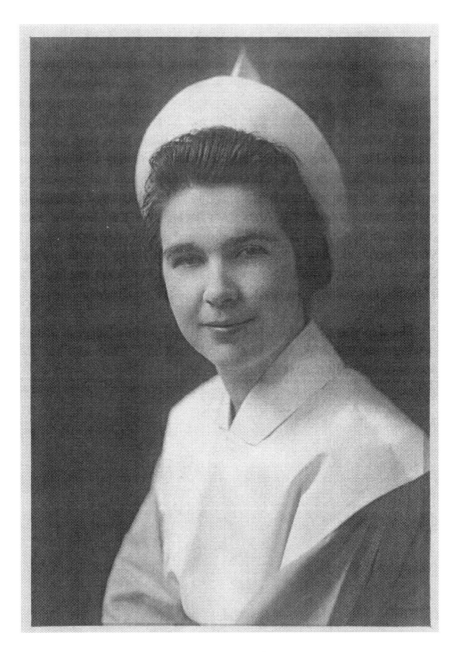

Mary Joyce, Graduate,
Mercy Nursing School, Chicago.

THE HACKLEY SMITHS

Mrs. Erie Hackley was the adopted daughter of a very wealthy lumber baron in Muskegon, Michigan, Charles Henry Hackley and his wife Edith. Erie was born in 1866 and married Leigh Barbour Smith in Michigan. He died in 1916 at the age of 50. . The Hackleys were great contributors "giving a third back" to the city of Muskegon... libraries, museums, and more. Time Magazine referred to the family as the "Medicis of Muskegan". Leigh Hackley Smith, a son, was born in 1896. We'll refer to him as "Hack" Smith henceforth.

It appears Mrs. Smith moved to the West Coast sometime after her husband's death. Leigh Hackley Smith is found in Portland, Oregon in 1915...when he marries Jeannette Bell Thomas (1891-1977). His wife isn't referred to again, so I suspect the marriage didn't last as Hack volunteered as an Ambulance Driver in France with the American Field Service in 1916 or early 1917.

Hack was one of 187 volunteers from Yale who pledged themselves to the French Army as drivers to transport the wounded from the front lines to medical services before the U.S. entered the First World War. Often under fire and later wounded, he served in the French Army's Section 8, which was taken over as SSU (Section 629) of the U.S. Ambulance Service when America became officially involved in the war in late 1917.

Most American drivers paid their own transport and living expenses while under French auspices. I don't know how long he served, but when wounded and in the hospital, Hack was given morphine, to which he became addicted. To further complicate matters, he also had a fondness for alcohol.

Mary Joyce in Hollywood, 1920's.

DISCOVERING ALASKA

In the summer of 1928, Mary was included in a trip to Alaska with Erie Smith and Hack, fulfilling a nurse-if-needed role. Hack, who was passionate about trophy hunting, his mother and Mary traveled to Juneau on the Smith yacht, the Stella Maris, skippered by W. E. Cox . The Smiths had been to Alaska a few times already. On this trip they surveyed parts of Southcast Alaska and adjoining areas of Canada, including the Taku and Stikine Rivers and Cassiar Mountains. Mary shot her first bear on this voyage at Freshwater Bay... but I doubt she loved this as a sport as she showed extreme fondness for all the animals that she encountered in the years ahead. She certainly appreciated the need for game as food and knew how to shoot and fish.

By 1930, Hack Smith had purchased a hunting lodge on the Taku River, know as Twin Glacier Camp, 35 miles by riverboat from Juneau and situated across from the awesome Hole In The Wall Glacier. I'd heard for years that Mrs. Smith apparently felt Hack would be safe from his addictions if he wintered over since no liquor would be available. The camp had been built by Juneau doctor Harry DeVighne in 1923 as a hunting lodge. His daughter raised red foxes. Fox are occasionally seen in the area today but I don't know if this was their origin.

The Smiths and Mary Joyce arrived at the lodge on the Stella Maris carrying lavender bathroom fixtures (of which the tub and sink are still in the lodge today), two pet dogs (a large white male named Skippy and Bug, a Boston Terrier) and a registered guernsey cow, Myra, because Mary hated canned milk in her coffee. Hack and Mary lived there year round... Hack was busy leading a crew building cabins and running trophy hunting excursions. They soon started raising sled dogs and were learning to live in the wilderness.

Mary took care of the dogs, the lodge, cooked, fished and helped Hack recover from drinking bouts in Juneau and from visits to cabins with stills along the Taku River. She also raised mink. For several months each year the river would freeze over...travel required dog team, snow shoes or ski plane, and ice skating was a welcome sport. There are pictures of Hack and Mary riding horses at Taku one summer, but I never heard her talk of horses up there.

As a chechako (Alaska newcomer) Mary was sent to get some fish shortly after her arrival at the lodge. She took Skippy, their large white dog, to help bring the fish back that she caught. She followed the trail to the creek she was told about, found the gaff hook hanging on a tree....it was used by anyone fishing there... and caught several large specimens. She loaded them on Skippy, but then decided it was only fair that she should carry half of them herself. On the way back, she was sitting on a log resting, looked up, and saw that a rather large bear was heading towards her and her fish. She had no choice but to shoot and luckily got to her rifle in time. I think the bear eventually wound up on a wall somewhere.

Until her death in 1943 in Los Angeles, Mrs. Erie Smith brought the yacht up from Seattle most summers, loaded with supplies for Myra and her offspring Moccasin and Mukluk. The cows wintered over at a dairy in Juneau.

Myra and her youngsters developed a strong appetite for salmon which found its way into the flavor of the milk. Salmon tugs of war with the dogs occurred, and Myra was found in the river, snapping at the salmon as she tried to catch one. Mukluk once got her horn caught in the dog's fence trying to get to their dinner, and it took hours to extricate her. She had an uncanny sense of smell and could ferret out the buckets of salmon meant for the dogs. Myra even made the cover of the August Alaskan Sportsman Magazine around 1939.

Early Taku Lodge, Mary Joyce
(standing above dog) with Guests.

Hack Smith died suddenly while in Wrangell, Alaska on August 13, 1934. Mrs. Smith deeded over the lodge to Mary Joyce, and continued some summer visits. Inventoried at the time at Taku Lodge were 15 sled dogs, 14 buildings and 3 cows. From my Wisconsin based family I had always heard that Mary was in love with Hack and I imagine that his death was very difficult for her. I never asked her questions about this because she never brought it up. I certainly wish now I had asked! Mary kept a lot to herself. (Later in her bartender days, she would walk back and forth behind the bar, taking in bits of conversations from talkative customers, many of whom were legislators... she knew so much about the people and the politics but I never heard her pass along any "secrets"...she simply did not gossip.)

She was alone now, but had a Tyrolean trapper caretaker, Louie de Florian, an individualist who had a cabin up river. He wasn't about to take orders from a lady even though he worked for her for about 10 years. They'd argue, Mary would fire him. He wouldn't stay fired. In September while catching, cleaning and smoking over 1000 pounds of salmon for the dogs' winter diet they often didn't speak for weeks.

The year after Hack died, in 1935, Mary started making plans for a dog sled trip she'd been mulling over...from Taku Lodge to Fairbanks, 1,000 miles of snow, ice, and untraveled trails. The Kluane to Tanana Crossing section was virtually unmapped - a place where whites had not yet been. She was covering routes that later became part of the Alcan Highway (Alaska-Canadian road built during WW11) She took off for her place in Alaskan history on Dec. 22, 1935.

*****

Here is that story of Mary Joyce, in her own words, written at the Taku Lodge on an L.C. Smith and Corona Typewriters Inc. machine in 1936. Such a typewriter is still at the Lodge today. I enjoy her wording and phrasing, so characteristic of the 30's. And her descriptions of the land and trails are exciting... her thinking on Alaska's progress, on women's lib, on acceptance of all people, on God and His creations, are put down on paper and wrapped in her wry humor. I did very minor editing of her manuscript: punctuating, an occasional word change, dropping a few paragraphs and newspaper articles that she had included at the end...and bracketed [ ] the few things I added for clarification.

Mary Joyce with Skippy in front of
Hole in the Wall Glacier, 1930's.

Getting Mail on the Taku River.

Wintering Over at Taku Lodge (Xmas Card, 1930's)

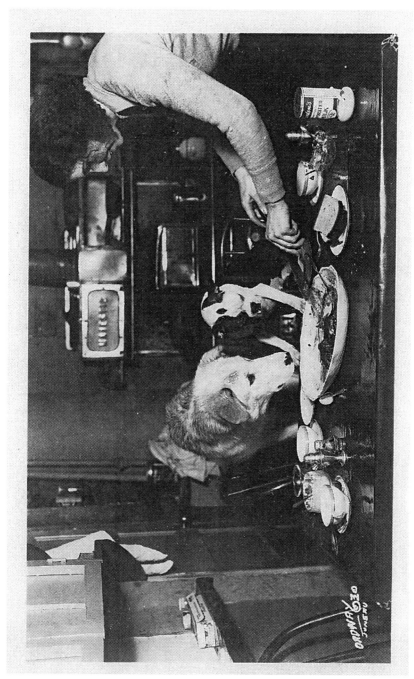

Mary Serving Supper to Skip and Bug
Kitchen of Taku Lodge.

Guests Inside Taku Lodge with Mary Joyce.

Leigh Hackley (Hack) Smith on
Basement Stair Stoop of Taku Lodge.

PART II . . . THE MANUSCRIPT

Mary Joyce and Dogteam Leaving
for Fairbanks December 22. 1935

CHAPTER 1.

1,000 MILES BY DOGTEAM

December 22, 1935. "I am going up the Taku River by dogteam to Fairbanks." "But you can't do that; there are mountains or something you can't get over. Anyway it's no place for a woman." Thus man disposes of woman. That settled I went quietly about my business of getting ready. Others roared with laughter. "Poor Mary...she'll be coming into Fairbanks two years from now, her dogs will be dragging her or she will be dragging the dogs. The dogs will eat her or she will eat the dogs before she ever gets there." Older men, more polite, simply shook their heads and remained silent.

If a man announced his attention of taking a thousand mile mush, certainly no one would think it strange, nor would his statement be greeted with roars of laughter. I as a woman resent the fact that men seem to think they should have the monopoly on all the fun. Is there any reason why a woman should not be as capable as a man? Anyway, I had planned on this vacation all summer and it looked attractive to me... everyone to his own tastes. I thought no more of going to Fairbanks by dogteam that you'd think of driving your car through the States, or taking a jaunt to Europe, except perhaps I'd have more fun. I had planned on going by way of Dawson from Whitehorse, however if I could follow the route of the Pacific Alaska Airways, it would be the shortest distance between two points. The pilots did not know if there were passes through the mountains between the headwaters of the Kluane and the Tanana rivers. It did not look very promising from the air, but Jean Jacquot at Burwash Landing on Kluane Lake would know. And so as the P.A.A. gives weather to all their pilots in Alaska, so now they placed all their facilities at my command, and they were many.

Jean Jacquot [from Kluane Lake] wired he had a guide that had gone part of the way. It was possible. His wife made a couple trips a year to Whitehorse by dogteam to visit their children who were in school there. I could meet her in Whitehorse and have company [for 200 miles] to Burwash.

The P.A.A. suggested I take a radio, but as I hardly knew the code [morse] and no time to learn it now, and wishing the operators to be on speaking terms with me when I got to Fairbanks, decided against it. I am only slightly acquainted with the dit and darr of a radio world. Besides I could not see myself climbing a tree to put up the antenna on a cold winter night. I was monkey enough, but not that kind of a monkey. There was to come a time when I deeply regretted my decision.

As weight is considered important in an airplane, so it is with a dogteam. Over a well traveled trail a dog is supposed to pull 100 pounds with ease, but my trails would not be traveled. And there would be stretches when there were no trails at all.

The essentials were:
-1 sleeping bag, supposed to keep one warm at sixty below with snow for a mattress,
-Silk Tent weighing 9 pounds,
-Small Stove weighing less that fitted into the basket of the sled and pipe that fitted into the stove,
-2 Pair of Snowshoes, large pair for breaking trail and a small pair fo follow behind the sled,
-Small Trail Ax,
-30-05 Winchester with case to kill moose and caribou for ourselves and dogs if necessary,

- Enough Smoked Salmon for 5 dogs for 30 days. As one can carry very little meat on account of its weight, one does not kill game unless absolutely necessary.
- My own equipment I'm ashamed to say weighed 100 pounds, and I thought I was going to be tough and travel light. I collected and discarded until there seemed to be little else I could discard.
- Fur Parka,
- 2 Pair of Ski Suits, one for everyday and one for Sundays,
- 2 Pair Corduroy Pajamas (I could not bear to think of sleeping In my clothes),
- 1 Pair of hip length Mukluks as they say it gets cold in the Interior,
- Half dozen Pair of Moccasins (they get wet and take a long time to dry out),
- Heavy and Light Underwear (it wasn't very cold yet),
- Dozens of Socks,
- Creepers for glare ice,
- Candles for light,
- Snowglasses, Flashlight, Tool Kit to fix sled and harnesses,
- First Aid Kit,
- Canned Heat for tea at noon when we didn't want to take the time to build a fire,
- And many other things I was to discard later along the trail as not important.
- My small vanity case was packed with a thermometer so I would know enough not to travel in weather below 40 degrees. At Dawson in the early days, the Mounties would not allow horses to work in colder weather - so why should I? One barometer so I would not get caught in a blizzard. Others have, but why should I when I was going prepared with all the weather gadgets.
- A Compass that a pilot had put on a map and with great pains and patience and for over an hour tried to teach me how to use it. It seemed quite simple while he explained, but was a different matter when I tried to use it. Why must magnetic north be 32 degrees east of north? Do you put north or magnetic north on

the lines running north and south on the map? I might end up at Fort Yukon instead of Fairbanks. "East is east and west is west"...why can't north be just simply north? Another man said "on account of the mineral in the country, you can't depend on it anyway." However there are times when a pilot's life and those of his passengers depend on his compass. If it was good enough for a plane, it was good enough for a dogsled. Besides it was really a nice silver and shiny compass, like a man's watch.

- Maps from Juneau to Fairbanks. Small maps and big maps. Plain maps and colored maps. They were really quite pretty. And not the least important ...
- In my Vanity Case was cold cream and cleansing cream. Woodbury's face soap - after all the ads say "It gives you that skin you love to touch." And Jergens hand lotion - if Walter Winchell is to be believed, "It keeps the hands soft and velvety" - perhaps even the hands on the handlebars of a sled. Powder, rouge and lipstick. A woman thus fortified should be able to conquer even the wilderness.
- But I was even better fortified: 5 pounds of beans, 5 pounds of rice, moose meat, 1 pound coffee. sugar, butter and hardtack.

CHAPTER 2.

TAKU LODGE TO TULSEQUAH

Finally on the 22nd day of December [1935], the river seemed sufficiently frozen for safe traveling and I was as ready as I'd ever be. Everything was piled on the front porch of the lodge and two dogteams were driven around for their sleds to be loaded. The team I was taking included Tip, Stikine, Nakinaw, Baldy and Taku. The other team of Inklin, Chesley, and Skippy, a large white dog and a pet, carried extra supplies.

I took a last glance around to see if I had forgotten anything, and a last good look as if to imprint on my memory as a picture on canvass the interior of my large lovely log cabin, with its huge stone fireplace and the trophies on the wall: the black bear from Oregon, the two grizzlies from British Columbia, the three brown bears from Admiralty Island, the caribou from the Cassiar [Canadian mountain range], the moose and goat from the Taku. Funny the way the goat looked as if he had socks on. Here one could spend a comfortable winter if one's feet were not so restless.

We got a late start but were only going 12 miles to the P.A.A. [Pacific Alaskan Airways] radio station at Canyon Island. The overflow on glare ice was hard on the dog's feet and some of them were bleeding. There were many tracks of moose and a hole where one went through the ice. I had supposed instinctively they knew enough to stay off thin ice - evidently nature had not taught them everything and I hoped I'd have better judgment. It was nearly dark when we arrived at the canyon but the fastest water on the Taku seemed now to be well frozen. From the howling of the dogs I realized other guests were here before us.

The Justice of the Peace of Tulsequah had come down to the radio station to report to Prince Rupert that a man had committed suicide in that district. He said "from the evidence it looked as if the dead man had gone down to the river's bank and jumped in - finding the water rather chilly he climbed out again, went up to his shack, took off his clothes, hung them up to dry, and put on a dry suit of underwear. Being comfortable, he took the butcher knife and slit his throat." The question seemed to be to bury or not to bury, with or without the sanction of the law. The citizens of Tulsequah were all for burying, but he wished permission to bury. The Justice himself had very little authority but the weight of it lay heavily upon his shoulders. As for myself it was none of my business. Let the Canadians decide their own law.

While I enjoyed a moose steak, the operator increased my appetite by telling me I would get lost and freeze my toenails on my way to Fairbanks. Why didn't I stay home and learn the code? If I spent just 15 minutes a day for one year in practice I would become an expert operator. Fifteen minutes out of every 24 hours; 7,554 minutes out of a year; 91 hours and 15 minutes out of a lifetime. It seemed reasonable enough, but did he know that at Fairbanks in the spring of the year they had an Ice Carnival that rivaled the Mardi Gras of New Orleans, the Tournament of Roses of Southern California? Didn't he know I must have "something to remember" when "I grow too old to dream"? There is no arguing with a woman and so to bed I went in the radio room with my big white dog at my feet. I suppose if I were to turn the switch, a ditt or a darr would jump down on my head. Most assuredly I must learn the code. Very sleepily I remembered I forgot my map. How does one get to Fairbanks without a map.

This morning after a hearty breakfast I sent my love and Merry Christmas greetings to Peg and Bob Ellis in Juneau. Bob sent back a hug and a kiss which Bob West thought undesirable to deliver on account of a month's beard. Bob Ellis said "it would only tickle her". We all left about 1:00 and Bob West came down to the river bank to see us off. My own two dogteams, with a man from my lodge driving one team, were accompanied by the Justice of the Peace, riding in the basket of his sled with a native boy at the brake, getting off from time to time to stretch his legs and advise me of the bad crossings.

Two hours took us to Tulsequah and here I delivered two months of their old mail. The main and only street is one block long, with the river bank on one side and small cabins on the other. Here the Tulsequah River empties into the Taku, and the Inklin River begins. And here I sat for four days, impatient to be off, while the white men argued that Inklin wasn't frozen enough...and the Indians argued among themselves. As I wanted an Indian guide, the decision of the Indians was more important to me. I knew one of the young Indians wanted to get to Atlin, perhaps as badly as I did, for reasons of his own. It would give him considerable prestige among his own tribe to take the first white woman over the Sloko Summit.

Christmas dinner was celebrated with a lovely roast of goat. Our host was an Englishman who had come into the Dease Lake country in 1898 but had never reached Dawson...so many of them didn't. Around his table were gathered prospectors and trappers, Indians and half-breeds. And I was the only white woman. After we had all eaten as much as possible, a delicious plum pudding was set before us whereupon a remittance man rudely pushed back his chair and shouted "I don't want any of that stuff!". Quite insulted he was...but perhaps if he had tasted the brandy sauce he might have changed his mind. He may have been afraid to mix a sweet with what he already had in his stomach...more than sourdough ferments in the old stone crock behind the kitchen stove. Anyway, he'd have none of it.

The day after Christmas the Indians decided, peacefully I hope, the young Indian would go with me and his father and brother would accompany us over the most dangerous stretches of the river. The father asked his son "can she walk on snowshoes?" and the son replied "I guess so...she's got two pair."

CHAPTER 3.

TULSEQUAH TO INKLIN HOUSE

December 27-29, '35. I was very happy to get started. Up until this time I did not know if I would be able to start for Atlin or have to go back home. My humiliation would be more than I could bare - it couldn't be explained. Skippy, my big white dog, was sent back (he is used to the luxuries of life) and two of the brothers.

The sled and the five dogs I was taking with me were loaded into a boat and we crossed the river. Baldy, the most timid of my dogs, was afraid in the boat but once on the opposite bank they all seemed as eager to be off as I was - although Nakinaw got in the basket of the sled and seemed undecided whether he would ride or pull. Perhaps he thought going to Fairbanks was a big joke, and I'm sure those on the bank thought the same thing.

Amid the barking of dogs and much wagging of tails, we finally got them harnessed and were ready to start when we heard a shout from across the river. It was the law of Tulsequah, "Would you be kind enough to deliver these letters to Atlin?". I would be delighted. The mail must go through, whether it be King George's or Uncle Sam's.

I had always heard of water as being blue, but for the first time in my life I have seen blue water the color of icebergs on the headwaters of the Taku. Blue water, fast, cold and cruel, running between its icy banks. We traveled on gravel bars, crossing the channel of the river on log sweepers with poles from the log to the bank on the opposite side. Chocack Lagoose, Billy Williams to you, scolded his two sons [Frank and Steve} and made them put boughs over the poles so I could not see the water underneath while crossing. "White lady plenty scared. She fall in river...we never get her out." I crossed on my hands and knees and the dogs followed like soldiers. We crossed the upper Taku another place over rapids on huge cakes of ice, three and four feet apart, held in place by sweepers and snags. They put a chain on Tip and as each dog fell in the water, they pulled him onto another cake of ice. Some of the cakes of ice were only two feet wide, just room for the sled, with water leaping over and gurgling underneath. I jumped over and just made it - but they had a chain on me too.

At night I cooked moose steaks, beans and rice. Rice with gravy on it. Rice with sugar and butter on it for dessert. Nothing like a change of diet. After dinner, old Billy Williams would tell us stories of the Taku in the early days, before the white man came.

Long before Juneau was ever dreamed of, when the Taku Glacier blocked the mouth of the river making a lake of the whole Taku valley, all the tribes gathered once a year for a potlatch at Tagun, on the headwaters of the Inklin. Here gifts and hostages were exchanged among the different tribes, and here for many days they carried on their wardance and merrymaking. They danced around huge fires, their own brown bodies flashing in the flickering light, each chief trying to out-do the other. These festivities didn't always end as merry as they had begun.

A story is told of a Chief, coming from far-off Wrangell, with 50 war canoes and 50 men in each canoe. As the King has his jester so the tribes have their song-maker, and he composed two songs for his Chief with which to woo the Princess of Tagun. As the Chief was singing his song and dancing round the fire, the Chief from another tribe threw some powder into the fire (perhaps the powder from a Hudson Bay shell) which exploded, throwing its burning sparks upon the Chief and his men. This being an insult from their host, the Taku tribe, war was declared and they entered immediately into conflict. The Chief went back to Wrangell with 1 canoe and 20 men. High on a sheer cliff I saw today in red Indian dye the picture of a canoe headed home. Above the canoe is a bleeding heart, and to the right is a moon high in the heavens, and the picture of a wolf (meaning the wolf, or Taku tribe) high in the sky, unable to be defeated. The ruins of many war canoes are still on the Taku and the skulls of many men remain at Tagun. There are many clans in each tribe. A wolf marries a crow. Their children take the clan of the mother who was a crow, and they in turn must marry a wolf. If they marry a crow, it is a deed punishable by death.

One of the Taku tribe killed an Indian from Sitka, but got an arrow in the back which wounded him. The Sitka Indians came to make war on the Takus but were paid in cash with the agreement that if the Taku died of his wound within the year, the money was to be refunded. He died. Whether it was a violent or natural death will never be known, and then the Takus went to collect their money back which was at first refused. However, before the war-whoop began, the money was refunded and peace was declared. These Indians were as clever with their bows and arrows as Read and Soapy Smith were with their pistols.

Tomorrow we reach the Inklin House, trapping ground of the Takus. The tent is very comfortable with its small stove. It was desperately cold today until we passed the "Den of the Northwind". My big toe got frightfully cold - I must have a hole in my sock. I was told to wear silk hose and woolens over them and I'd never get cold. The Indians say "no good" just the same as they say "fish no good for dogs...meat more better" so they killed a moose on the river. There is no doubt but what dogs get more savage on meat, but I still think that on account of the oil in fish, it is...more better. Just the same as before I started out I couldn't bear to think of sleeping in my clothes, so now I can't bear to think of taking them off...besides, I have always hated to get up early. Now I don't mind because I'm dressed anyway...perhaps I only hated to get dressed. Long after I had blown out my candle and crawled into my sleeping bag on a mattress of spruce boughs, I could hear old Billy Williams laughing and joking with his two sons in their lean-to beside an open fire. They are the happiest race of men I have ever known with only the bare necessities of life, the sky for a roof. With all our luxuries we are never content and continually grasping for more. Our greedy hands reach out to snatch their silver foxes, and give them in return a bottle of lemon extract or a plug of star tobacco. We who send our missionaries to teach them might well learn a lesson in return.

CHAPTER 4.

INKLIN HOUSE TO ATLIN

December 31, 1935-January 7, 1936. Here the Nakinaw empties into the Inklin and the Inklin branches off to the northwest toward Telegraph Creek. From the Inklin House we traveled to Canoe Landing on the Nakinaw river, the end of navigation by boat. We followed the ice on the bank of the river with fast open water on one side. I had just taken some movies and had not strapped my camera on the sled when it hit an ice cake. Before I could grab it, the sled tipped over and my movie camera bounded into the open water. Frank was ready to dive in after it, but they finally made a gaff hook of poles and fished it out.

From Canoe Landing, Billy and Steve Williams went back and I started up Sloko Mountain with Lakuta Sladanta, otherwise called Frank Williams, with his sled and two dogs carrying smoked salmon and my Woods sleeping bag. My own sled was so heavy that in steep places we put seven dogs on and both of us pushed and pulled.

The first day of a new year, and as your feet danced on hardwood floors to the music of many orchestras in many cities, mine danced up the side of Sloko mountain to the music in my own heart...and if the music had not been there, only then would it have been a hardship.

We took turns breaking trail. It was very hard work for me to find the blazes of the Indians, as they do not wish them found. However when I went ahead I took an ax and blazed a trail that a white person might find - if anyone cared to pass this way again. Every time I hit a tree, the snow would fall down my neck. The days were dark and cloudy, but not cold.

I took three days to reach Sloko Summit and glorious sunshine. As I stood on top of this mountain I could see hundreds of ptarmigan raise in flight from the peaks of other mountains, looking like a cloud of snow blown by the wind. Suddenly I hear the roar of another and more powerful bird, and soon see the silvered Electra plane winging its way to Juneau. I wanted to reach up and pluck it right out of the sky. It was an intrusion from my own world - I too, with my dogteam, was presumptiously intruding into a world I knew nothing about. But there in the plane were boys I knew. If I could only feel the clasp of their hands and hear the sound of their voices. I was quite indignant they didn't drop down to reassure me. There seemed to be many landing fields and the terrain was cluttered with lakes. As the roar of the motor died away I realized I had left my own world behind - the modern Alaska with its airplanes. I had gone back to the old with its dogteams. But in this world of white madness, the wind was beginning to blow and I decided I'd better get along before the Gods became angry. Here on a mountain pass was no place to get caught in a storm. There was a time and a place for everything and here was no place for dreams.

We dropped down to Silver Salmon and the protection of spruce trees, crossing the old Telegraph trail to Faulkners cabin, three miles south of Dixie Lake. Had I come this way two years before, I might have met the mail teams on their way from Atlin to Telegraph Creek. Now the mail is carried by planes. Here was a trail Tip knew well, born in Telegraph he led his brothers over this trail with the mail when he was only 6 months old. Although it was only two o'clock in the afternoon, it gets dark at three. I would not move a step further. Here was a cabin, although the windows were out and one could see between the logs. It had no door, but there was a roof under it, and it had a small stove with an automatic damper. When the chimney got red hot the damper would close. To keep warm one had to rotate continually. When I sat on the stove, my feet were cold and when my feet were warm, the rest of me was cold. Wherever Mr. Faulkner was tonight, I blessed him for building this shelter on a spot where he was forced to stay out in a blizzard because he couldn't make the next cabin.

Frank went ahead to break trail and I cooked supper and fed the dogs. Nakinaw wanted very badly to come into the cabin. One night on Sloko mountain when I was unharnessing the dogs, Nakinaw's feet seemed so cold he could hardly stand on them. He kept lifting one paw and then the other. I thought perhaps they were freezing and I took him into the tent to get warm. He lay on my sleeping bag and took what food was offered him. After I had blown out my candle he had an idea where the moose steaks were kept and proceeded in that direction. I had to crawl out of my warm bed and tie him outside. It was a mistake I did not make the second time. He howled for two nights in protest.

It did not take long to cover the trail Frank had broken the night before and soon we were in deep fluffy snow again. Frank went ahead and I hopped, skipped and jumped to pack the snow down so the dogs could pull the sleds up the hills. I'd take one team up the hill then go back for the other. My approach was always greeted with enthusiasm on the part of the dogs. I hurt my shoulder lifting and pushing on the handlebars. They say the man who drives the dogs is the biggest dog of all. There are times I think they're right. Long after dark, as we were trying to make Hot Springs on the O'Donnell Road, we came to a farm. The light from the window looked so good - my hands were so cold, toes blistered from snowshoe straps, and my shoulder ached.

I rapped on the door and a voice demanded "what do you want?" "I want to get warm" I said in a very small voice. Was this the northern hospitality I had heard so much about? I also wanted food and shelter for myself and dogs although I did not suggest it.

It seemed an inopportune moment to do so. Soon two eyes glared out from a glass opening and the voice demanded "who are you?" Who am I? I mumbled something. He had me stumped. How was I to tell him who I am when I don't know myself. It's a question that has long been a question mark in my own mind. Who are any of us? It seemed ridiculous standing out there in the dark and the cold to explain to him that I just happened to be one member of the human race that inhabited southeastern Alaska, a Territory of the United States. Evidently there was no such doubt running through his own mind. "Go away you nobody" - a fact I knew but hope no one suspected. I should have been delighted to have it explained in so many words and so definitely, but I was furious. Soon fear followed indignation and I got away in a hurry. I had heard of men going crazy living alone...of course some go crazy living with someone. After I got out of rifle range, I laughed heartily. Learned later the old man had extended his hospitality to others, and got two black eyes for his generosity. We mushed on, dogs' tongues hanging out and crawling on their bellies through deep snow. I felt very sorry for them until we came to fresh moose tracks when they cocked their ears, curled their tails, and all I could do was to keep them on the road. There are times when I think I have a bunch of hunting dogs instead of sled dogs.

After my encounter with the old man, my hands were no longer cold and I felt very happy. It was as if a load had been lifted off my shoulders. The result was even more satisfying than if I had warmed my hands by his fire. It really was quite funny. I shall never forget how his eyes protruded under very heavy eyebrows, and his head was very shiny where his hair should have been. There was a moon coming up...I have never seen trees so beautiful. We traveled a trail of fairyland, with each twig on every bough covered with frost and ice, and every tree an artist's model.

Reached Bruce Morton's Hot Springs at eight o'clock. Here I stayed on the road and sent Frank in to see if we might stop overnight. I wasn't going to be turned down twice in the same night. From the road I could hear him shout "white woman wants to stay all night".

Perhaps there was a catch to it after all. Must it be explained I am white? What color am I supposed to be? It must have been the pass word because I heard "bring her in". I was received with open arms. This must be hospitality...how gorgeous - warm fire, warm house, warm food. I sank into a chair. It seemed to me as if I could never walk again. How my legs ached. After you have followed an Indian for 25 miles all day through deep snow, you know you've been someplace. They are born on snowshoes.

Mrs. Morton gave me two pair of woolen mitts she had knitted herself to put under my moose-hide mitts. One pair was white and fluffy, reminding me of a kitten I had as a child. She warned me to always keep one pair in my belt, near my body so they'd be warm and dry to put on after the sun had gone down. "Your hands perspire during the day, and that's why they get so cold at night. Stupid of me not to have known.

White sheets and a pillow. I put the pillow carefully on a chair. Who invented the bed? Certainly mankind didn't give him enough credit...what greater service has been done for humanity? I felt like the man in the Insane Asylum who when asked why he was hammering his hand, replied "it feels so good when I stop". I too love to sleep in my tent but it feels so good when I don't have to.

I was asleep when my body hit the bed. A few hours later I was rudely awakened by dogs barking. I sat up in bed and listened intently. One can tell by their barking if they are fighting among themselves or barking at something. The result being if they are merely barking, I don't have to get up...if fighting, I have to get there as soon as possible with a stick before they kill each other. It seemed to be neither. I couldn't distinguish this sound, but as it kept on I couldn't sleep anyway. I looked out the window into a clear moonlight night and saw a horse chasing the guide's dogs around the trees where they were tied. He would first go after them with his head, and then turn around and kick up his heels, always being careful to be at a distance where he couldn't reach them... very thoughtful of the horse, a colt of 15 summers frolicking in the moonlight. Had he been chasing my dogs, I would have gone out and given chase to the horse.

The next morning I suggested I ride the horse to Atlin, but they said he was unridable. I wondered if they have ice cream in Atlin... but they don't...funny that I should crave it so. We started up the middle of Atlin Lake but had to hit the bank on account of slush ice and arrived there early afternoon.

CHAPTER 5.

ATLIN TO WHITEHORSE

January 13-19, 1936. I remained in Atlin six days, mainly because I couldn't seem to get filled up. I was perfectly fascinated with the amount of food my guide could put under his belt on the way here, and now I was eating more than the guide. I'd no more than finish a big meal and I'd be hungry again. I wondered if there wasn't a limit to my capacity, but there didn't seem to be.

I purchased a small four foot saw, thinking it would be safer sawing my own wood that it would be chopping it. From here my guide, Frank Thomas, was going back and I was going on alone to Whitehorse. My load from here on would be much heavier and I realized I should have a toboggan instead of a Yukon sled...but there were none to be had.

There seemed to be very little activity in this small town - the mail plane from Carcross being the big event. I left Atlin with the feeling that I didn't want to stop in any more towns. It seemed so terribly depressing when I had been so happy on the trail. I heard over again all the gruesome stories I had ever heard about the North. From all I could gather the people thought I was crazy, until I began to think maybe they were right. Surely I couldn't be the only sane person among so many insane. I decided however if I was the only one crazy, it was a happy state of mind to be in. If they wanted to sit by the kitchen stove all winter and knit, that was their business. I can't knit. It's a pastime I will leave for my wheelchair days. I know it is very unreasonable for me to feel this way.

A whole town should not be blamed for the thoughtlessness of one man who seemed to know more than all the others combined, and as I think of each individual it is with kindness. But must I be made to die a thousand deaths until I am dead? Must my feet be frozen off my body while I am still alive? I wish to dance again.

In contrast to all this were the lovely messages I received from Juneau. Here were friends who had known me a long time. The Pacific Alaska Airways offered every assistance and would keep an eye on me on their scheduled runs from Juneau to Fairbanks. There were people who wished to help instead of hinder, with constructive advice instead of destructive... with their assistance I need not be afraid. I could rely on a pilot's judgment and so I sought it. He gave me a map of his own and marked the mileage and the roadhouses I would come to along the way. He gave me credit for having a reasonable amount of intelligence and did not push me through the ice until I had fallen in. I was deeply grateful.

I left Atlin determined to stop in no more towns. I did not want people to take my happiness from me...it was too precious. Alone in God's glorious sunshine, its rays seemed to penetrate my heart and lift my spirit high into the Heavens. How wonderful to leave man's depressing atmosphere. I headed North traveling on the lake, the dogs clipped along at a merry pace, and my heart sang. Six miles out of town I was overtaken by two motorcycles, two boys on each car. The dogs nearly bolted. They had never seen anything on two wheels before, or heard the roar of a motor. One of the boys tried to pet the dogs and Nakinaw made a grab for his hand. Alaskan sled dogs are one-man dogs and personally I would never think of walking up to a man's dogteam and trying to pet them. It's just not done. Winter sport on Atlin Lake - hunting coyotes by motorcycles.

Supposed to travel 20 miles and come to a roadhouse on the right bank of the lake. I'd followed the Indian trail in the middle of the lake all day, it's nearly dark and I can't see the cabin so I decide to hit the right side and pitch my tent. As I get closer I think I see smoke, something is moving...man or moose? I shout and am shouted back at. Napolean Champoux, a man of 68, helped me unharness the dogs and feed them.

Next morning I had breakfast at six A.M., waiting for day to break but it never did. I harnessed the dogs and started across Atlin Lake in thick fog. I thought I should follow my own trail back to the middle of the lake, but Mr. Champoux said he would take me there...he went ahead, but pretty soon we were headed straight back to his cabin. I was well pleased. I thought if an old sourdough couldn't make it, certainly it was no place for a chechako [newcomer]. And they told me I most likely won't be able to find the portage anyway, which is a road joining Taku Arm and Atlin Lake, over which they carry freight from Carcross to Atlin by caterpillars in the winter time.

The next day dawned bright and beautiful. I followed the moon going down in the west, like hope in the human heart, now dimmed by clouds, now bright with glory. To my right was the head of Atlin lake, stretching away in the horizon to misty blue distant mountains. Outlined sharply against a northern sky stood the mountain of Minto, round and white as a woman's breast. From out of the east, a flaming sun peeks over the tips of jagged mountains while to my left and south, the city of Atlin...silence, save for the padding of dogs' feet on frozen snow.

Three miles of this and I hit the soft fluffy snow through the woods. Tip broke trail for his team and only his back and head could be seen above the snow until he became too tired...then I broke trail ahead on snowshoes, coming back each time to lift the sled out of the snow and push. The sled kept turning over. I continued this all day until an hour before dark when I realized I couldn't make the roadhouse that night. Only covering a mile an hour all day, the woods of the portage still ring with my blessing, heaped on the head of the man who invented sleds with narrow runners. After crossing a small lake and pitching my tent I found the only dry tree on the portage and chopped my wood for the night.

I had the stove all ready to light before I unharnessed the dogs so if my hands got too cold I could start a fire easily. The harnesses are so cold. I fed the dogs and cooked rice and tea for myself. I did not get supplies at Atlin because there are roadhouses all the way to Whitehorse. I just didn't make the roadhouse. Usually on the trail one carries rice, beans, salt, sugar, tea and there are plenty of rabbits and ptarmigan or moose. You can't imagine how good a grain of rice can be especially with a little butter and sugar on it. The bean for breakfast is just a bit hard to get down, but once having come in contact with the stomach, one can travel for hours without getting hungry.

I crawled into my sleeping bag and waited for the wolf to come, but he didn't show up, even in sheep's clothing. I didn't dare put out the thermometer for had I known it was 40 below I would have frozen to death. It's a dry cold up here...one doesn't mind it.

It seemed even colder in the morning. I started the fire from my sleeping bag and made tea. After harnessing the dogs and dumping everything on the sled, the dogs were frantic to be off, and raced down a hill and onto a lake. There were three big moose across the lake. The dogs wanted to go in their direction - I wanted them to go in another. I finally won and two miles down the lake we came to the trail of a trapper... had wonderful going to the next roadhouse where I stopped at noon. It was cold. Every time they opened the door I felt like shouting "please close that door", just like Sam McGee.

The next day I traveled north again on Taku Arm to Tagish Lake. The Arm running north and south gets the full benefit of the north wind which sweeps the snow off. I crossed the boundary line, passing from British Colombia into the Territory of the Yukon.

Suddenly I hear barks and snarls, and looking across the lake see half a dozen large animals coming out of the woods and coming my way. Oh dear, and they told me the wolves would get me. My knees began to shake as they do sometimes at the dual controls of an airplane. There's never anything I can do about it...only hope the pilot doesn't notice it...but he always does and one feels so silly. I grabbed the gun and wondered how I could hold it steady and then I heard "mush godammit mush". I put the gun very quickly into the case and hoped I'd stop shaking....despite the fact that I had investigated all the wolf stories of the North and there's no instance of wolves attacking man.

They will attack dogs if they can lure them off alone, and they will follow a dogteam for miles. They're afraid of the scent of man and are the biggest cowards in the world...and so am I.

Made Butterfield's Roadhouse at dark and it was bitterly cold with a north wind blowing. The dogs were put in a nice warm barn, out of which I had to take Tip half an hour later lest the brothers tear him apart. He tries to put them in their place and they resent him. I discovered both Mr. Butterfield and I had wandered far from our native homes in Wisconsin, and we visited until midnight.

Only 12 miles to Carcross, traveling west again on Tagish Lake. No poor words of mine could possibly describe the beauty of this morning. The sun flaming red in the east...white sharp tips of mountains suspended in the clouds...purple snowfields on low rolling fields...azure icefields floating down into the sea. I'm as jealous of this country as a husband is of his wife. I wish you to share its charm and beauty. I do not wish you to possess it. And someday it will all be spoiled by man. Herds of men and women will drive out herds of moose and caribou. I'm glad to have seen it before it becomes cluttered up with a lot of funny looking people.

I was afraid to go into Carcross but I arrived there at one o'clock and had lunch. There was nothing wrong with my appetite. I called at the post office for my mail, and the postmistress told me to come back in half an hour and her husband would give it to me...yet she was the postmistress but evidently her husband did the work. It seemed quite funny.

I went to the telegraph office and had a nice chat with the operator. I was ready to make a dash for the door at the least mention of the perils and the terrors of the trail, but none were forthcoming and he did not question my sanity. Carcross is not far from Atlin, but the people seem different. A Canadian Mounted Policemen came in, tall and very handsome in his coat of scarlet, and he asked me to have tea with his wife and him. It was delightful, people with merry laughter.

He told me of inspection trips he had taken by dogteam and we compared notes on the grub box, which after all is most important. I laughed until the tears rolled down my cheeks about rice and beans. I drank many cups of tea and ate all his wife's delicious cookies. How friendly these people are...perhaps after all, towns will be all right. I lingered one night at Carcross then hit the railroad tracks for Whitehorse, passing deserted, tumbled down railroad stations which reminds one of the fact that rather than a new country, this has known the days of '98 [goldrush]. I crossed two high bridges, the space between the ties seemed wide enough for me to fall through. Tip stopped in the middle and stood looking down perfectly fascinated. I kept shouting "whoa" all the way across, with my toes turned out and my heels turned in, running on the rail. I reached Robinson Roadhouse, 22 miles, in six hours...fairly burned up the tracks. People ask me if I ride...of course I don't ride. The dogs didn't ask to go to Fairbanks, I asked the dogs...and if they are gentlemen enough to pack my baggage, I should be willing to pack myself.

Left the next morning at 9:30 and reached Cowley before noon. The operator at Carcross had telephoned ahead to keep the men with handcars off the tracks lest they run me and my dogs down. Miss Enright had lunch waiting for me...first time I've eaten lunch on the trail. But they can't fool me about clearing the tracks for me...the day was that of the Sabbath.

I've now been following the railroad tracks for two days. It seems an endless afternoon to get to Whitehorse and it's almost dark now. I get frantic if I haven't pitched my tent, or reached a roadhouse before dark. The wind started to blow early afternoon and has gathered speed toward evening. Finally came to the canyon, now with the howl of the wind I hear the roar of the Yukon. I see a suspension bridge across the river, and I have that complex...I can't stand to look down from high places. It's dark and the dogs might break a leg. I will not cross another bridge, especially one that wiggles under me with that roar in my ears and cakes of ice clashing and grinding below. After an eternity I see what looks to be a roadhouse, but tracks to the left of me and tracks in front of me end in snowploughs. Houses across the river, which way to turn? And then two figures emerge out of the darkness and come up to me. "Where is Whitehorse?" "Ten miles farther on." By his wit I knew him to be one of the P.A.A. operators. We turned to the left, he took the handlebars, and I ran ahead of the dogs into Whitehorse and stopped in front of the Whitehorse Inn.

A man came out. "Let me see...where we put dogs?" What did he mean "where we put dogs?" Here in the North they are used so much. "Oh no...not much anymore. Everything carried by plane." While he was trying to think I whispered "where is the manager", and was told he was the manager. I was quietly subdued.

I have to have them near the hotel where I could feed them...also to settle their disputes if they had any. We drove around to the back, unharnessed them, and put them in an old shed after removing the old buggies, scrap iron and whatnot.

I wondered why they kept looking at me and finally one of them said "but you're not at all what we expected...we thought you'd be big and masculine and you're so little." I told them "I'm sorry to disappoint you, but I'm afraid I'm as big as I can ever hope to be." There was much laughter and friendliness. I felt immediately that I had known these people all my life. The lobby was comfortable and charming with large chairs and tables, and as I warmed my hands by the open fireplace, it was almost as if they had all put their arms around me and drawn me close to their hearts. There was no criticism nor curiosity in their glances.

A member of the Yukon Council asked me to their "Curling Games". My education has been sadly neglected. Misunderstanding his English accent I thought he said "Cuddling"...Oh you do that in Whitehorse? I told him I was willing to try anything once. He was tall and dignified and everyone laughed merrily. Three Mounties

ROUTE TAKEN BY MARY JOYCE ON HER
1,000 MILE DOGTEAM TRIP FROM TAKU LODGE TO FAIRBANKS,
1935-36.

dropped in to say hello in their scarlet coats. Are these the men that get their man? And they answered "or whatever we go after". They looked like boys fresh from college, but perhaps those merry blue eyes can be cold and stern, and those arms handle a horse and gun. I drew myself up and put on my dignity. I had been warned against "Scarlet Fever" in Whitehorse.

Ron Greenslade, the operator, said "you'll have to hurry...we're going out for dinner." Warm room and a hot bath, how good I felt. On our way over to the home of our host it was explained to me that he was an ex-mounted and had spent years in the service. There are many of them around Whitehorse. They serve in the North and are then sent outside where they resign...for after having seen the ice go out in the Yukon for years, they are lost. They must come back, although at the time they think they never want to see this God-forsaken country again.

Candles flickered on the table and silver gleamed from a snow white cloth. Civilization again. My host asked me if I were going to Dawson. "No, I'm going by way of Kluane." "I don't think you'd better." I stood on two feet and glared at him, while he stood on his and glared back. Out of flashing eyes he measured me and I measured him. Then I do not know what passed between us, but I liked him immediately. It was as if we had shaken hands.

Dinner was announced. A huge turkey was set before my host. My eyes nearly jumped out of my head. Turkey in the Yukon, the 19th of January, there must be some mistake, how did he get it here. I don't know why it surprised me so, but before I could accept some turkey my mind had to travel the bird's route to the table...back to Skagway on the coast, and up the White Pass and Yukon railroad to Carcross and down the tracks I had been on for two days. My mind having arrived with the turkey I was quite willing to eat him and all his trimmings...and ice cream at last.... My hostess was an American who says she keeps these Yukoners in their place by telling them "We won the War". Her husband says she's won all battles ever since. Their 22 year old daughter went outside [the lower 48] last summer to stay a year and came back in a month...but then the operator might have had something to do about that. For the week I was in Whitehorse the doors of this gracious home were open to me both day and night. They'd take us home after a party, feed us and send us off to bed. When I grow older in years, I hope I may be as young as they are in spirit. [You were, Mary!]

CHAPTER 6.

WHITEHORSE

January 19-25, 1936. Sunshine - cold brisk days - snow crunching under one's feet - log cabins and modern buildings. It all seemed to lay so peacefully under winter's blanket of snow. The river, white and still, yet with that feeling of expectancy as if one were always looking for something. People eager and alive.

Huge red barracks fill a whole square block, weather worn and windows out. Large enough to house a regiment but no longer needed. There are no lone prospectors coming from Dawson with pokes of gold to be waylaid by murderers who made this their business. And in this building is the scaffold. I looked up with horror...here men were hung by the neck until they were dead. It seemed a terrible retribution, but they had no compassion for their victims. How can a bright and shiny metal make such beasts out of what is supposed to be man.

I've seen the cabin of Robert Service's Sam McGee [Cremation of Sam McGee] ...the door was locked but I peeked in at the window.

"And there sat Sam, looking cool and calm, in the heat of the furnace roar, And he wore a smile you could see a mile, and he said 'Please close that door'."

I walked up to the Whitehorse Rapids and wondered how a boat could ever get through that mad, white whirling water leaping over boulders, and now turned to a jade green on the ice below. It looked so cruel. On the bank of the river is a log cabin dedicated to Robert Service, and a guest book where many names are written. I couldn't restrain from putting my own name down and adding "Taku to Fairbanks by dogteam or bust."

I talked to the children in school who were far more interested in my dogs than they were in me. I realize I would have made a bigger hit had I driven my dogteam into the schoolroom, but what would the teacher have said?

I visited the hospital and talked to three old prospectors from Kluane way. "My girl, you have a tough trip ahead of you. One glacier to go over in which many lives have been lost, between Kluane and the Chisana." A glacier was something I positively would not go over. I can get cold enough without sitting on an icecap. "I'm going in a straight line from Burwash Landing to Tanana Crossing, the way the planes fly." "But no white man has ever been that way before. There is no trail".... the country is filled with.... tall bunches of grass, where you have to jump from one to the other, and if you missed you fell in mud and muck up to your waist. They sounded like the bogs of Ireland my grandfather used to tell me about. Well perhaps they would be frozen over - at any rate they would be covered with snow and there was an unusually heavy snowfall over the whole of the North this winter. I have known the buck-brush of British Columbia, the devil-clubs of Southeastern Alaska...I must know this clump-grass of the Yukon.

I had tea with the Sergeant and his charming and beautiful wife. What is it about this country that puts a merry twinkle into the eyes of all men. Is it the "strange sights they have seen" or do they know the "secret tales of the Arctic trails"? However men that have danced with a madwoman, going outside with an escort in their best uniforms and boots on the sandy banks of the Yukon must have some sense of humor. It may be only the reflection of the Northern lights or stardust from the cold bright stars.

I climbed up the hill to the landing field. God must have looked far ahead when he carved this perfect table, high above the Yukon... from the days when men, scantily clad, broke their hearts to get to Dawson, toiling long days of weeks and months [searching for gold] in an unknown country to the boys today in woolen ski suits, fur parkas and mukluks who land here in a few hours from all parts of the North.

Joe Crosson and Walter Hall fly down from Fairbanks in the Pacific Alaska Airways Lockheed Electra, dipping their wings in salute over Whitehorse and going on to Juneau. A message from Walter Hall...tell Mary Joyce it's a hell-of-a long ways to Fairbanks. And he measures distance by mountains and lakes and rivers at 180 miles an hour. I measure those same mountains and rivers at 25 miles a day on a good trail. Maybe he's right.

Vern Brookwater with the big tri-motored Ford of the White Pass makes three trips from Skagway with freight and passengers. Bob Randal with the Pilgrim of Northern Airways comes in from Dawson just at dark. It's 40 below and a strong wind blowing. I dash out to help him turn its tail into the wind, put wood under the skis, tie the wings down, cover the motor and drain the oil. It takes longer than unharnessing the dogs and one's hands get just as cold. Flying during the winter months in the north is not all sitting in a warm cockpit. He carries perishables and case after case of eggs to Dawson. I wondered what would happen if he had a forced landing. He'd be all over the eggs, or the eggs would be all over him.

I have seen the snowmobiles and caterpillars take off for Dawson towing three or four bobsleds loaded down with freight. The caterpillars replaced the horses and go about six miles an hour. Now the snowmobiles are replacing the cats, and can make from 10 to 12 miles an hour. There are two drivers who take turns driving continually both day and night. Passengers are not catered to. If you wished to spend the winter in Dawson, you should have been there by this time...however, if you missed the last boat, you may have an air-conditioned deluxe apartment on top of the freight. This is an accommodation I do not believe you are charged for but it most likely will be taken out of your hide. Personally I'd rather go by dogteam, or take my chances with the eggs...they at least make a good shampoo.

Whitehorse in the moonlight...stars twinkling in a blue heaven ...northern lights flashing across a clear cold sky...diamonds dancing on a field of snow...one Mountie to the left of me and one to the right. We walked down to the river's edge. The old stern-wheelers, large white river boats covered with snow, seemed so out of place there on the river bank. What relation could they have to this white frozen river? I asked "what do you do in Whitehorse all winter...no shows?" "Curl...just simply curl" they echoed. Stupid answer and more stupid question. But what could they answer - I can't answer it myself. What is it in this land that grips our hearts and will not let us go?

"No shows?" There's a show in Whitehorse every day...

- The young Indian that freighted for Bryant Washburn on Kaskawulch Glacier comes in from Kluane Lake with his dogteam, but minus one ear. It seems the dogs got into a fight and in parting them he fell down and one of the dogs bit his ear clear off. Not content with that, the dirty dog swallowed it, or he might have kept it frozen and had the doctor sew it back on. Everyone laughed heartily and thought the poor dog had very slim pickings...except no sympathy in the Yukon.

-The handsome young officer from Teslin, 300 miles away, arrives with his dogteam... black fur cap tied under his chin, striking fur parka, beaded moose moccasins up to his knees, beaded caribou mitts up to his elbow. An Irishman in His Majesty's service, he told me "the greatest hardship I ever had to endure on the trail was when I ran out of marmalade."

-A young man fresh from England asked at the Northern Commercial Company "which are the warmest...snowshoes or moccasins? The clerk replied "snowshoes of course." "I'll take half a dozen pair"

- A new Customs Officer was being trained on Lake Bennett. In checking over the outfit of an American, he came across a double-bitted ax and shouted to his superior officer "hey, your honor, here's a bloody bloke trying to cheat the customs with two axes on one handle."

One night we all snowshoed two miles up the hill and across the landing field, through the woods to a log cabin to dance until 3:00 in the morning. A Japanese lantern lit the doorway, lighted on the inside by an open fireplace and candles shielded by artistic shades with scenes of the North, moose and caribou. We danced in ski suits and moccasins to the tunes of "Isle of Capri" and "Jingle Bells". This must be romance, and if you wish to be popular in the North, put on your own snowshoes and make sure that they stay on. Not that our men are not gallant...they are, far more than any I have ever known...but if you make a nuisance of yourself, there are times that you'll get left at home. While it's not always necessary to keep your own hands warm, at least be capable of doing so.

Whitehorse was not all play and no work. Every day I cooked huge amounts of cornmeal and tallow for the dogs. They were beginning to get restless and straining at their chains. Every time I entered the barn their paws would come up on my shoulders. I was told quite sternly I pet them too much which is considered poor etiquette in a dog musher... but I like friendly dogs out of whose eyes gleam love rather than hatred. I also wish to get to Fairbanks in one piece, and I want the dogs to have as much fun going there as I am having. They tell me I will be the last one over the trail, that dogs are done. So long as the North stands for romance...so long as there are hearts that dream, dogs will never be done. There's a thrill to driving a dogteam found in no other sport. Though you cannot sing a song, songs will be sung in your heart - though you cannot write a poem, poetry will be written on your soul.

I exchanged my Yukon sled with its narrow runners that bury themselves in deep snow, for an oak toboggan. I would have preferred birch because it is so much lighter, but didn't have time to have one made. The handlebars and brake were transferred to the toboggan. The Indians seldom used either, but I like something to hang on to and one can help guide the dogs around trees. They put raw moose hide on its bow which stuck up in the air about two feet so if I hit anything, it wouldn't crack the wood. It looked like an old Spanish Galleon.

The most important thing was food for the dogs and light that can be carried on the sled. One can not cook dog food on the trail. I went over to Taylor and Drurys and they brought out what looked to be sheets of cardboard, and yet resembled the skin of a fish. What manner of salmon is this? It had a most unpleasant odor. My mind went back to the Taku, to the fat red Kings, bright and silver out of icy salt water. A dog will stay fat all winter on half a salmon a day. I examined it as one does a piece of material, turning it over and over. It seemed to be of good quality, what there was of it. "Is this the best you have?" "It's all we have." "But Whitehorse is on the Yukon... surely the salmon run up the Yukon." "My DEAR girl, you are at the headwaters of the Yukon which travels northwest from here til it touches the Arctic Circle, and down toward the west to the Bering Sea, hundreds of miles away." I felt like a small child whose parent was explaining why I could not play with my best doll today because it came from China, many miles away. It dawned on me that if the poor fish had to beat his way up the Yukon from Norton Sound, across the whole of Alaska, and into one of England's colonies, no wonder his bones were broken and nothing was left but the skin. "I'll take 50 yards and tallow." A dog must have fat, especially in the winter time, to keep him warm.

Wires from New York to Fairbanks warned me "Go by way of Dawson. Do not go by Burwash Way." But why...I must know why. "Because there is a broken trail to Dawson and shelter cabins all the way - because from Burwash to Tanana Crossing there is no trail, there are no cabins." But didn't they know I had a tent and stove... there was no trail over the Sloko Summit.

The parting of the ways, the highway or the byway. The highway led to the north; the byway led to the west. To the north, a broken but long and lonely trail, with Dawson 400 miles away. To the west, a broken trail and two traveling companions for 200 miles of the journey to Burwash. From Burwash Landing to Tanana Crossing, what? I did not know, but knew I must find out. If and when I got to Tanana, I would be practically in Fairbanks. From Dawson, I still would be a long ways away.

They have made the road to Dawson sound so easy that anyone could do it, and if anyone could do it, why should I? Now while my feet are young, let me know the unknown trails. When I grow old, I shall go knitting in a wheelchair down the road to Dawson. There is perhaps no human being more stubborn that a woman, unless it's a man. I couldn't go by Dawson now even if I wanted to. The west held a fascination for me that I could not resist.

"The trails of the world be countless, and most of the trails be tried;
You tread on the heels of many, till you come where the ways divide;
And one lies safe in the sunshine, and the other is drear and wan,
Yet you look aslant at the one trail, and the lone trail lures you on.
And somehow you're sick of the highway, with its noise and its easy needs,
And you seek the risk of the byway and you reck not where it leads."

Anyway, who are these pilots from Fairbanks, sailing the uncharted sea of the sky, out of the blue and into the fog who are advising me. It's as if you said "do what I say, not what I do." Was there fear in your heart as your chin grew more determined and your black eyes flashed through the fog at Point Barrow. You were only over the Arctic Ocean. Nice landings.

How about you ...did you swallow the cigar you were chewing because you could not light it in the plane, when the sky jumped out from under you and you fell 2,000 feet. "What would I have done had I been in the hood?" Did you bump your red head when you crashed through the ice at Telegraph Creek? Was there fear in your heart as you flew across the Bering Sea and into Siberia? Fear for your friend perhaps?

Are you all so eager and alive today because tomorrow you may be dead? You are not afraid to live but you are afraid to die. One walks with head held high and proud perhaps to hide the fear and terror in one's heart. You who lead the way tell me not to follow.

I've lingered in Whitehorse a week. My toboggan is finished. I seem to be filled up and the dogs leave part of their food. I have gone over my outfit and things that seemed very important at first do not seem so important now, so I'm sending my sled and 100 pounds over the White Pass Railroad and back to Juneau. It perhaps still is a long way to Fairbanks and although I had hopes of getting there before the ice goes out in the spring, I had no hopes of getting there for the Ice Carnival on the fifth of March... but despite all the warnings, the people have been very encouraging.

We danced at the Whitehorse Inn Saturday night until midnight, had supper and danced until dawn. The others went home and to bed. "We'll see you off at 7:00 a.m." I knew if I went to bed I wouldn't get up, so I packed my baggage and lashed my toboggan as day was breaking and the Northern Lights, like balls of fire, hurried across the sky.

I went through the corridors calling very softly for the manager, and finally in desperation called very loudly. After all, I could go without breakfast, but I couldn't very well leave without paying my bill. They might say "she left between two Suns"...it's a reputation in the North one can never live down. He finally awakened and I paid my bill, had toast and coffee, and hit the trail for a rest.

CHAPTER 7.

SAFARI BY DOGTEAM
WHITEHORSE TO BURWASH LANDING

January 25-February 4, 1936. Mrs. Jean Jaquot, wife of the big game outfitter at Kluane Lake and Clyde Wann, who brought the first plane into the Yukon, each driving five big malamutes, called for me at the Inn. I brought up the rear and we galloped down the main street with all the stray dogs of the town following us, disturbing the Sabbath morning with their barks and howls. We soon left a sleeping Whitehorse, and if I have taken a bit of your hearts with me, I am leaving you part of mine in return.

Bright sunshine filled the world, lighting up the peaks of snowcovered mountains and painting them every color of the rainbow as we traveled up one hill and galloped down another. At noon we built a fire and had hot tea, hardtack and cold meat. Lunch is a luxury I never permitted myself before, but now the days are longer and we travel a greater distance. Nothing ever tastes as good as hot tea on the trail, and we had a very good trail. In this land of airplanes it is surprising how many dogteams are driven by prospectors, trappers and the Indians. I suppose the day will come when trapping and prospecting will all be done by planes.

The dogs keep up a steady trot all day. I can't walk and keep up to them but every time I jump on the toboggan their heads turn around and their brown eyes look back at me with reproach. I tell them "well look, the others are riding"... and they seem to say "you've never ridden before, why should you now?"

They are no doubt spoiled, but I am so accustomed to walking now I almost prefer it. Besides, it's good for one, and I do get a chance to ride down the hills without them knowing it...otherwise it's mostly a dogtrot all day.

There are cabins with stoves in them every night to stop at, and huge barns for the dogs. They used to use horses over this road hauling freight to the gold mine at Chisana. So all we have to do is chop wood for the night and leave kindling for those that come after us. And woe be the man that does not leave kindling if he is found out. It's an offense not tolerated by the Royal Canadian Mounted Police. It has saved many a man's life.

I thought I was pretty good on the trail for a woman until I traveled with Mrs. Jacquot [aka Pete]...but then she is better that most men. It keeps me hustling doing my share and keeping up with them, but my reputation depends on it or next time I may find myself traveling alone. Everyone has his hands full taking care of his own dogteam.

Each day is gloriously beautiful, new mountains to gaze on, new rivers to cross. There is much wagging of fifteen dog tails, and much laughter and gaiety among ourselves. I wish that everyone might know the joy of this. The temperature stays around 20 below, just right for traveling without a parka.

Two and a half days took us to Champagne. I was a quarter of a mile behind the others...I can't resist stopping my team and gazing around. The others have seen these scenes before and are likely to again but as I can't take them with me, I must enjoy them now and, as far as possible, imprint them on my memory. I do not want to lose them. I climbed a small hill, and down in the valley below me were perhaps a dozen log cabins with smoke curling up from the chimneys...and my companions unharnessing their dogs in front of one of them. Above these cabins on a high plateau stood perhaps two dozen miniature modern houses, painted white with blue or green shutters and doors and red roofs. It resembled what might be a child's Utopia, standing so beautiful and bright in the sunlight.

I took some pictures and the dogs were becoming impatient. Cabins usually meant a rest for them and lots to eat, especially cabins with smoke coming out of their chimneys. I thought I might miss my own lunch, so jumped on the sled, put my foot on the brake and we dashed down the hill. Soon the dogs were unharnessed and after lunch huge amounts of cornmeal, tallow and fish were cooking for them. We decided to remain the next day to rest ourselves and the dogs.

Champagne has two trading posts and the last postoffice I would encounter for some time to come. My load was still heavy. I took everything off the sled and dumped it on the floor. If I didn't need all this on the trail, I would want it at Fairbanks. Skates, I should like at the Carnival; extra ski suit as I might go through the ice. I finally got a box and after filling it, it weighed 50 pounds, which I sent back to Whitehorse to be taken to Fairbanks by plane. My load from here on consisted of the bare necessities of travel.

The next day I fed the dogs twice and wandered around. There are two white men here, one Mountie and the agent at the trading post. I walked up to the doll houses and my Utopia turned out to be an Indian graveyard, with everything in them the occupant might need in the happy hunting ground of the hereafter, even to snowshoes. I decided snow-shoes might be an optimistic thought in anyone's hereafter...I hope I need them myself.

That night we danced in the combination trading post and postoffice. Any event is an excuse for a dance in the Yukon. A huge stove in one end, and on shelves and hanging from walls all kinds of trappers supplies: guns, traps, snowshoes, moccasins, sleeping bags and other necessities. In the warehouse behind, bales of this season's furs were beginning to accumulate: muskrat, beaver, mink, cross and silver foxes, and a few immense wolf hides.

The agent for Taylor and Drury was about to buy the best looking pair of riding breeches in the store until I told him they were girl's. He asked me how did I know. I told him if he didn't know he was too young to learn. He said "If you determine the sex of the breeches, I will buy". After all, he gave me potlatch for my dogs. One good turn deserves another and I perhaps saved him from future embarrassment.

Dancing with the Mountie I warned him not to bump into that other couple...looking around he saw no one else dancing and asked me if I came all the way from Taku just to kid him. I told him I'd kid everyone I could. I was the first white girl they had danced with for months, but daybreak comes early and I had 25 miles to dance the next day. Today dawned clear and warm, with a temperature of 20 above, too warm for traveling. We had not left Champagne far behind until we were all mushing along barehanded, bareheaded, and in very light sweaters...and still the perspiration rolled down my back. The dogs were very lazy only coming to life when they saw a rabbit jump across the trail and Pete (Mrs. Jacquot) shot it with a twenty-two. They all hoped they'd get it for dinner that night.

About two miles from each roadhouse we would stop and cut small dry trees and pack them on the toboggans. The trees around the cabins have been cut down long ago. Many times there were long hills to go down and although I used dog chains, and lashed the wood as tight as possible on top of my load, and then tried to steady it with my body, they would start rolling and I often landed at the bottom of the hill in a snowdrift.

We were all very tired that night. It isn't the trail that's killing me, it's the night clubs in your cities. The temperature dropped in 24 hours from 20 above to 15 below, which was more to our liking. I was very anxious to see Bear Creek Summit but I had been warned not to come over it alone. I was wondering if it would be anything like Sloko Summit. It was a small winding mountain trail we climbed in a few hours. However one looked down a thousand feet and had to keep the toboggan turned on its side to keep it from slipping. There were no trees to stop one if it started rolling.

There was a heavy ground fog which felt cold and damp. We left our caps and mittens on. Mid-afternoon I wished I had my parka on and late afternoon I executed this wish although one's hands get cold while doing it and usually one is too warm afterwards. In my journey so far I have found a fur parka too hot for traveling unless one rides all the time.

The second night out we arrived at an inhabited roadhouse. It seemed wonderful to go into a warm cabin, no wood to chop, no food to thaw out and cook. The dogs were fed on caribou and they needed it. Here I learned how to mush dogs from a man that had done it for 30 years...after all, one should learn something in half a lifetime, although I did wonder why he protruded so far in front. He went to Los Angeles and brought back a school teacher. She was a very good cook too. She told me what she had given up to come to the Yukon...electric lights and stove, hot and cold running water, steam heated apartment, and a Plymouth. I remembered the Chrysler roadster I had left in Los Angeles to exchange for a dogteam in Alaska, and none too soon. I had been arrested six times in the last two months I was there. It was very unlikely I would ever be arrested for speeding with a dogteam in Alaska.

We visited a trapper and a few Indians were camped nearby. The next morning we left at 9:30 and had gone only a couple of miles when my dogs began to growl and I heard something behind me. Looking around I saw two dogteams and called softly to Clyde Wann "There's someone behind us". He gave one look and shouted at the top of his voice "Hey Pete, the savages are coming." I was completely startled and didn't know whether to defend myself or not...I had not heard of the Indians being savage since my schoolbook days.

Mrs. Jacquot was aways ahead but I saw her turn around and heard her voice ring out "they'll go ahead" - she stopped her team and hollered "you go ahead". They hesitated for a minute and then put on their snowshoes and swung their teams out around me for a minute, and back into the trail ahead of her. It had snowed a couple of inches and their going ahead would make it easier for us, and they had no loads as we did...although I did feel quite sorry for them. If I had been told to go ahead by Mrs. Jaquot I would not have hesitated. She can pick a hundred pound dog out of a dogfight and throw him into a snowdrift as I would a rubber ball. An Indian will camp on a trail for a week at a time waiting for a white man to break trail for him. He's not in a hurry, he isn't going anyplace.

Later in the day we caught up with them and Mrs. Jacquot went ahead and they swung their teams in behind me. My dog Taku didn't much like another dogteam behind him. He uncurled his tail and seemed afraid they would pounce down on top of him. I noticed it increased his speed and he wasn't pulling much today anyway. I'm told that when a dog doesn't work you're supposed to beat him, but I never do. If he doesn't work today, he will tomorrow...just so they don't all decide not to work the same day. There are days when I don't feel like working myself and I would resent a beating terribly.

The affair with the Indians in the early morning kept me in gales of laughter all afternoon. Every time Clyde looked around I tried to straighten my face. I was afraid he would not know I was laughing with him instead of at him, not that I think he'd give a damn.

We arrived at Kloo Lake early afternoon and stopped at a small trading post... there were several small cabins around. The village is built on top of a glacier. You don't believe that...neither did I until I dug down a couple of inches and struck ice. The trader was expecting us and had cooked a huge caribou roast with browned potatoes, vegetables, and lots of gravy. I'm ashamed to say we ate nearly all of it, and I could hardly move to feed my dogs. I slept on the floor in the store on a mattress of bear and wolf hides and it felt heavenly.

We left at 8:30 the next morning after a hearty breakfast. Ten below and a black sky above with a few blue pockets. Came over Boutterlier Summit which was quite like Bear Summit, except the trail was very badly drifted and straight down in places. The toboggan kept sliding, and although a cold wind was blowing the sweat ran down my back. We arrived at Silver at the south end of Kluane Lake at 5:30...25 miles in eight hours, having taken 1 hour out for lunch. The wind was drifting the snow so we couldn't see the trail a few minutes after we'd been over it. We started a fire in one of the cabins and after cooking supper, went visiting. A trapper had just come in with his dogteam and it seems a fox got caught in one of his traps and before he could stop his team, the dogs were on top of the fox...not wishing the pelt to be torn to pieces he tried to get to the fox and got tangled up with the whole mess...man, fox, dogs. The fox reached up and got the man across the bridge of the nose and under the upper teeth. Round 1 went to the fox.

There are three or four white men here and a couple dozen Indians. One white man is married to an Indian woman..they have four children - one a daughter about 16, tall and slender whose eyes gleamed like black diamonds under straight black eyebrows, dark hair and bronze skin. She looked very beautiful sitting at a small table reading by candlelight. I walked over and asked her what she was reading. She held up the books and after glancing at them and then her surroundings, I wondered what there could be here to satisfy the soul of a girl who read Keats and Shelly, but perhaps that's why she was reading them.

The wind howled all night but died down at dawn. We traveled up the lake all morning and entered a small cove at noon to fix our lunch at the cabin of an Indian woman. After lunch we started out again intending to stop all night at the cabin of a white man farther up the lake which we reached at 3:00. Both Pete and Clyde said they didn't know if they could stand it. "Stand what?" "The odor of the cabin. He keeps mink and cooks their food inside." I told them I had smelled mink food cooking before, and many other disagreeable odors. I could stand it if they could for a warm place to sleep.

They drew up in front of the cabin and stopped their teams. I halted mine behind their sleds. A man came out and they went into the cabin with him...a few seconds later they came out. Clyde came back to me and said "go have a sniff". "What do you mean, have a sniff...you are getting pretty finicky." I walked in to warm my hands and closed the door after me. But I couldn't warm my hands. What was it? It hit me in the face and nearly knocked me down. This wasn't mink food...mink food is bad enough, but not this bad. This was something I've never smelled before. I couldn't put my finger on it but I was curious enough to want to diagnose it. I determined to take one more chance and took one more breath. It didn't seem to be any one thing, more a combination of all the most disagreeable odors I have ever smelled in all my life. It wasn't decent, it attacked from all sides to penetrate one's whole body. I felt that I couldn't live if I took one more breath and so stumbled to the door. I can stand a lot, but not that. I looked around to see if there wasn't an old barn we could stay in, but realized if we did stop here, we'd have to stay in the house. Mrs. Jacquot told the man she thought we could make Burwash that night; there would be a moon...and God's fresh air.

We went on for a couple miles, but it was getting dark, the dogs were tired, and 20 miles to go. If we unloaded and went in with empty sleds, we could perhaps get there by midnight, but then we'd have to come back for our baggage the next day. "Might just as well hit the timber and camp for the night." Clyde asked me how big my tent was ..."Nine by seven I think." When he unfolded the rag house he said "it looks more like a two by four." We tied it between two trees and set up the stove. Clyde chopped the wood. I carried it in and started the fire. Pete fed the dogs and collected our sleeping bags, cooking utensils and food. We all moved in...there didn't seem to be much room. I most likely was off a couple of feet in each direction in my tent size estimate. We sat around the stove on our sleeping bags, with our backs against the walls of the tent. After thawing out our food, we cooked and ate it. They kept stuffing the stove with wood and said they couldn't get warm. I moved back into the farthest corner and finally moved outside to get cooled off. I must be getting used to a rag house.

The next morning after taking down the tent and loading our supplies, we left at 10:00. The thermometer registered 18 below and it wasn't long before we were out of the bay and the shelter of spruce trees. We had to leave the right bank and travel up the middle of the lake and here we got the full benefit of the northwind. To reach Burwash we had to head into this howling gale... the alternative was to cross the lake and hit the opposite bank...but then we'd only have to retrace our steps and the distance would be too long. The dogs despised it...they don't mind going with a blizzard, it helps them along... but they hated a head wind like this, and so did I. I thought my nose would freeze and drop right off. The wind whistled through the space where my socks hit me below the knees and my parka hit me above the knees. I kept rubbing my cheek that turned toward the northwind.

I had once seen a man with a white nose and chin, and two little patches on his cheeks. I asked what was wrong with his face and was told it was freezing. He looked so like a clown I had to laugh... I did not wish to arrive at Burwash looking like a clown and tried to keep my head below the sled. My knees had long since ceased to be cold and were just numb, but they seemed to function and I kept hitting them with my hands. There was no excuse for this. I had hip length mukluks in the bottom of my sled, but it had seemed so warm there in the bay. I finally grabbed a pair of moccasins out of the hind sack on the handlebars and tried to tie them around my knees, but they wouldn't stay on. It seems moccasins were made for feet, not knees.

After we'd been out in this a couple hours, a sort of beard of frost and snow a quarter inch thick formed on our faces and eyelashes so that now my face seemed no longer cold and I felt quite warm. Another hour took us to a point on the lake where we turned toward the west. The wind now swept by the hood of my parka. We were no longer heading into it, and there was Burwash in the distance. Something was flapping on the lake and the dogs started after it. They thought it was a coyote to chase and I jumped on the back of the sled. The coyote turned out to be a flag...there were many of them marking the landing field on the lake.

Coming into these P.A.A. radio stations is like coming home to mother after a long journey...it was my only contact with the outside world...like receiving letters after many months. Jean Jacquot [Pete's husband] and the operator Red Wadell came to greet me and told me to go in and get warm, but I wasn't cold then; only after standing by the fire in a warm room did I begin to shiver. It was two o'clock. We had only been out four hours and had covered twenty miles. It seemed much longer.

We were all famished. Jean had a roast of sheep waiting for us, seasoned as only the French know how. It was my first taste of sheep... I had been told it was more delicious than any other game and I was not disappointed. Whitehorse to Burwash - 200 miles - nine days traveling time and it's 60 below tonight.

Mary Joyce in her Trail Gear

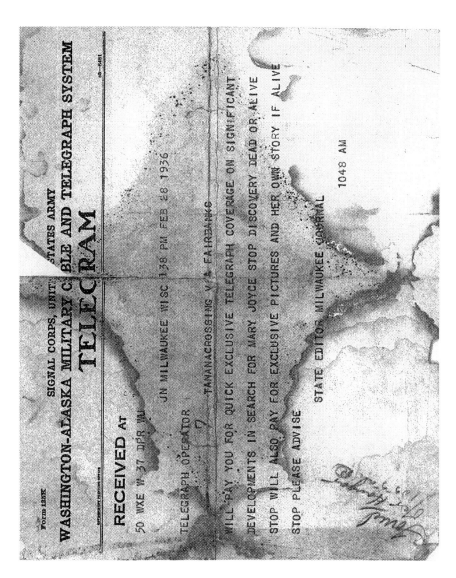

Wanted Dead or Alive Telegram

BURWASH LANDING

You will not find Burwash on the map but it is situated on the northwest end of Kluane Lake. It is a small village by itself. From here Jean Jacquot starts his hunting parties, big game hunters from all over the United States and Europe bag their game here and go back home to brag about it to their friends. They pick the largest heads from herds of caribou and moose, climb mountain peaks for the largest ram, and perhaps shoot a bear on the way home. While their friends only see a beautiful mount hanging from the wall, they see the colored rock on the walls of the canyon of the Donjek. A smile plays around their lips, lines of care leave their face and they're again telling stories or singing songs around their campfire, with the sun going down in the west, blessing them and bathing the world in its glory.

From here I could send messages to Canyon Island which were relayed 12 miles to my own home on the Taku. I received wires from Juneau to Fairbanks. Messages of encouragement and cheer. Masterpieces of wit and humor. If they thought I was going into the wilderness to be lost they gave no indication of it, but told me of trading posts I could look for on the headwaters of the Tanana. I wanted to tell them if I were lost in getting to Tanana Crossing not to look for me, but I didn't have the courage. I did tell them I would not travel if it got below 45 degrees. That's what I thought.

I cooked gallons of cornmeal, oatmeal, frozen white fish and bear fat, which looked like huge slabs of bacon for the dogs. The bear fat seemed to do them more good than all the rest, although on the third day Tip turned up his nose at it. The brothers gobbled everything they could get and like myself, never could get enough. Jean has the only cows I have seen since leaving [mine on]the Taku, and I drank 3 or 4 glasses at a meal. I crave milk and ice cream more than anything else. After the second day, the cavity which was my stomach seemed to be quite satisfied after a workingman's normal meal.

For two nights it has been 60 below, and would warm up to 40 below during the day. I was more than comfortable in a log cabin with a stove, although I had to break the ice to wash my face in the morning. On the trail we all washed in snow. My toboggan needed fixing so Jean and Steve strung it up on beams with a heavy weight in the middle and put the hump back where it was supposed to be...I'd lost it someplace on the trail. We took the sleigh bells off the dogs harnesses so we could get caribou or moose if we needed to, and to compensate the dogs, we put huge red pommels on their collars. Pete says "they travel much better that way" and they did look striking against the dogs' black glossy coats.

For a year little Jean Jacquot, age six, had imitated [pilot] Jerry Jones. He wanted to walk, talk, and look like Jerry. I could hardly blame him...Jerry is something to look at as he steps out of the silvered Electra in his uniform of blue. But Jean's idol came crashing down last summer when one day Jerry stopped on his way to Fairbanks with his family Eileen and Gail. He asked his mother "Why did Jerry Jones go to San Diego and buy himself a girl and baby?"

The fourth day young Jean packed my grub box and in spite of my protests, besides the old standby of rice, beans and meat, he added bread, a large pound cake, marmalade, and other delicacies. We had also cooked a large mulligan. The temperature the last two days has been around 30 below, and minus 40 at night. The extreme cold seemed to be over and not likely to occur again. Everything was loaded on the toboggan...tent, stove, sleeping bag, gun, our own food, and all the dog food we could pack. I left my large pair of snowshoes here, I was told I wouldn't need them...that [my new guide] Jonny Allen [and his dogteam]would break trail. All I'd have to do was ride. It sounded easy, too easy. The next trading post was Snag, on the White River 150 miles away.

Mary and guests in boat on Taku River
across from Hole in the Wall Glacier

CHAPTER 8.

BURWASH LANDING TO SNAG

February 9-16, 1936. The dogs were brought out and harnessed. They seemed to have more pep than they'd ever had before... perhaps it was the bear fat. My weight on the brake would not hold them and Red Wadell hung on to Tip. It was 30 below and we had 25 miles to go to the trapping cabin of Allen. Red let go of Tip, I lifted my foot from the brake, shouted "all right" and we dashed out the gate and around the corner. When it seemed safe, I turned and waved a quick farewell.

We had broken trail and soon were on top of the hill in a clearing, and here the wind was blowing. It had seemed warm enough in the valley without a parka but I needed it here. I took off my mitts, pulled it out of the lashing and with one foot on the brake and much difficulty in holding the dogs, got it over my head. By this time my hands were quite cold. At noon, Allen built a fire, melted snow and made tea.

We followed the bank of the Kluane River, the most dangerous river in the Yukon, fed by warm springs which keeps it open in places all winter. The trail was so narrow that boughs rushed at my cheeks on either side. Every time the toboggan hit a tree, gobs of snow would come down on my head. Early afternoon I was running behind a toboggan on whose handlebars I could hardly keep my hands...in and around trees and sometimes getting wedged between them. I became very hot....the toboggan rolled back and forth [across clumps of dangerous grasses] like a ship in the trough of heavy waves.

We arrived at Allen's cabin before dark, unharnessed the dogs, unloaded the toboggans, and while I built a fire he got rabbits out of his snares and set them again. He then lined rabbits and caribou around the stove to thaw out for the dogs. We ourselves had sheep chops, bread and gravy, and rolls and marmalade for dessert...and as usual, much tea. The thermometer registers 45 below and the barometer is rising. Sky clear and stars bright. [a rising barometer indicates calm, clear, colder weather; a dropping reading means cloudy to stormy weather.]

February 10, 1936. This morning it is 60 below. Over coffee I suggested "perhaps we should not travel today"...merely an echo from my own thoughts, but Allen replied "70, 80, all same" and was ready to go. I knew of course people did not travel in weather this cold unless they had to, and that this would be the coldest weather he had ever been out in. I had no desire to stop myself on the second day out of Kluane unless absolutely necessary, and if he could take it, so could I. On my shoulders depended the prestige of the white race.

If we could make 30 miles today we would come to the trapping cabin of Tom Dixon and it wouldn't be too bad to have a cabin to stop in. I had to stop three times to warm my hands before I got my toboggan lashed, and I was able to only harness two dogs when I'd have to dash into the cabin to warm them again. One cannot do anything in mitts and gloves that are not warm.

I pulled the wolverine on the hood of my parka as close to my face as possible and we left at 9:00 a.m. The fog raising from the open Kluane was so thick I couldn't see Allen 50 feet ahead of me. We had to go very slow, the dogs were coughing, their coats were white, their breath looked like puffs of smoke from a chimney. I experienced the greatest difficulty in breathing, each inhalation felt like the sharp edge of a knife cutting my lungs. The sun came out about noon, which made traveling much easier.

There was fresh snow on the trail which made the toboggans pull hard and we finally put on snowshoes and walked ahead of the dogs. We were now following a trapper's trail on the headwaters of the Kluane River. The sun went down and it again became very cold. We traveled on and on, bend after bend on the river. It started to get dark. I wondered if we would ever come to the cabin. "How much further?" "Couple miles."

We'd go a quarter of a mile to the west, a bend, and then a quarter of a mile to the north. Two hours later we must have covered at least six miles. "How much further...are you sure you haven't gone by it?" "Couple miles, not far now." I had not minded 60 below too much, but I did mind 60 below on a river in the black of night. More bends...I could not see them but I knew we turned. I could barely make out Tip at the head of his team, and finally I could not see Taku directly in the front of the toboggan. We were on the edge of the river with huge cakes of ice piled up which made the going very rough. I held on to the handlebars and thought if I do fall between the cakes, perhaps my snowshoes will catch and hold me up. I took the flashlight out of the hindsack, but the battery was frozen and it wouldn't light. By this time I couldn't even see the sled and I gripped the handlebars tighter. I could hear the water rushing under the ice. I hoped the dogs knew what they were doing because I didn't. I had long since ceased asking questions...I now knew what a couple miles meant. I also knew, whether or not we had passed the cabin, our only hope lay in keeping on the move. It was too dark and too cold to put up the tent and chop wood. Suddenly I felt slush beneath my feet, the toboggan turned to the right and we were going up a steep bank of the river. We had arrived.

I said I would not travel if the thermometer got below fifty and I never dreamed of traveling in the dark. I had done both. And now that we were in a warm cabin I forgot my terror on the river. It's 60 below, the barometer has gone up 15 points since morning. It's the first time Allen has been on showshoes all winter and he says "my foot hurts and I'm tired." I may be tired, I don't know or care, I only know I'm glad to be here. Glad to be able to feel another emotion rather than the dumb despair I experienced on the river.

I tied Taku away from his team to give him the advantage of a doghouse but evidently he'd sooner be cold than be away from his brothers...so I had to get up at midnight and put him closer to them. Allen slept the sleep of the very tired, and I kept the fire going all night...only toward morning did I fall into a deep sleep and did not wake up until 8:00.

February 11, 1936. After a hurried breakfast and leaving a note for Tom Dixon thanking him for the use of his cabin which we had helped ourselves to, we got away at ten o'clock. It was 48 below, and the barometer had dropped five points. I was both interested and fascinated by the sensation of my hands in the process of getting cold. There seemed to be three distinct stages. No matter what the thermometer registered, it always seemed colder in the morning. I would roll up my sleeping bag, we would then tear down the tent and stove and start a fire outside. I would then start to lash my toboggan. First my hands would feel cold, then they would be cold... from this stage on they started to ache, and when I thought I could no longer stand the aching they would pass into a sort of numbness. When I could no longer use them, it was time to warm them. And the whole process was reversed in thawing them out. It was much easier when we had a cabin to stop in.

We were now off the river and we traveled through the woods. We built a fire for lunch, melted snow and made tea, which always tastes more like spruce that it does tea. We crossed the Donjek River shortly after lunch. I kept up a steady dogtrot helping Taku around trees and through the scrub brush. My hands and shoulders perspired even in this cold weather. It was too cold without a parka and too hot with one. Never have I followed a more crooked trail or a rougher one.

We hit the bank of the Donjek again. Tip went to the edge and looked down...space seems to fascinate him. I tipped the toboggan on its side and as we passed I had no desire to look down. The loose snow and cold is hard on the dogs feet. They ball up and the dogs lie down and bite it off. None of their feet are bleeding however.

The trail led through thick underbrush and for two miles seemed more like a jungle...vines so thickly interwoven one couldn't see a patch of blue above, and in many places we had to crawl under on our hands and knees. It seemed very good to get out of it. High mountains on either side, unknown and unnamed by a civilization.

We had hopes of meeting some Indians that were trapping in this district and now came across their cache on the trail, although they had not been here for some time. We traveled on and came to a trail that branched off toward the west and written on the snow was "Wolf Mountain".

This information for my guide was like a signpost in the wilderness. We wanted to find the Indians and get meat if possible. We were running short on dog food. The other trail lead toward the north and we didn't know where the Indians were camped.

Allen decided to shoot off his gun to get their attention. I was standing near my dogs, Baldy and Taku, who are desperately afraid of gunfire...the others are looking for rabbits or a moose. Allen pulled the trigger and more smoke seemed to come up in his face than up the barrel. I dashed forward to see if he were hurt but he was only scared. I must take better care of my guide than he does of me...after all he could get along without me, but I'd be lost without him. A tiny part near the bolt had snapped, perhaps because the gun was so cold. We listened for an answering shot but didn't hear any.

We kept on toward the north and came to a small lake. The dogs smelled caribou tracks, put their ears back and took off down the middle of the lake. I had more sense of speed that I've ever had in a plane. We arrived at the head of the lake and found the Indians' tent.

They came back after dark from trapping.

Never was one white fleecy cloud more welcome in a blue heaven than the one that appeared toward evening, only to disappear into a cold bright starry night. However it's warmed up to 40 below and the barometer is dropping.

February 12, 1936. The Indians had killed two caribou the day before which I bought from them. We were getting low on both our own food and dog food. I stayed in the tent while the Indians went for the caribou and Allen went to break trail. I developed a perfect passion for the thermometer and barometer, and saw the temperature rise from forty below at six A.M. to 16 below at six P.M. The barometer dropped 15 points during the day. We could hope for warmer weather and I was glad to see a gray day.

February 13, 1936. The barometer seemed to creep up on me during the night and actually dropped down again so it was 40 below when we left this morning with a caribou and a half to the good. In spite of the trail Jonny had broken the day before, the going was hard for the dogs...they kept breaking through and I wore snowshoes. If possible, the scrub brush became scrubbier and the clump grass nastier. The dogs would jump on a log, and down again. I would lift the bow of the toboggan onto the log. The dogs would pull, the toboggan would balance in mid air and slap down with a bang, and I would go over after it less gracefully on snowshoes. Around trees and behind trees I'd pull the handlebars this way and that. Suddenly the bow hit something, the handlebars swerved to the right, and the toboggan fell over on its side. I must have had a very tight grip or my mitt caught on the sled, because my arm seemed jerked from its socket, and I was pulled off my feet and thrown into the snow between two trees. I felt dizzy and very sick to my stomach. It was the most terrifically sudden pain I had ever felt in all my life. Tears sprang to my eyes and rolled down my cheeks...but girls do not cry on their way to Fairbanks, especially if there is no one around to hear those cries and the tears felt very unpleasant and froze on my cheeks. I gathered myself up. I had not seen Allen since early morning. I wasn't even sure I was on the right trail. Miles back, one trail had branched off to the left...I hoped it was the trail to the caribou kill. Tip had followed this trail and I had relied on his judgment. Now I had only one arm to go over and under logs. I went on and on and wondered what I'd have done had I broken a leg. I finally caught up with Allen who had tea ready. It's wonderful what a cup of tea can do, even for a helpless arm.

As if to compensate for the rough going of this morning, we came to a frozen winding mountain stream and followed it up Wolf Mountain. We took off our snowshoes, rabbits darted across the trail, the dogs became alert and started to run. We camped beside the stream at 5:00 P.M. and I was delighted to see a cloudy sky. It's only zero degrees, and the rag house seemed nice and warm tonight.

February 14, 1936. From here on I became disinterested in the thermometer. It was 14 below and cloudy, warm and snowing slightly, but I'd sooner have anything but that extreme cold.

We followed the mountain stream and reached the summit of Wolf Mountain at noon. Going down the other side of the mountain, the ice was thin, and we had to hike through the woods. We put on snowshoes and Allen went ahead, very slowly and seemed to limp. I asked him what was wrong with his foot, and he said it hurt. I told him I would break trail and tried to, but my small trail shoes would bury themselves in the deep snow and become lodged in the scrub. I'd have to reach down and pull them loose with my hands. I couldn't even go as fast as he could and cussed myself for leaving my large pair of snowshoes in Kluane.

We traveled along the bank and on the stream when possible. There was no trail and the trees and brush were very thick. We made very poor time. Towards mid-afternoon we hit the stream again, crossing from side to side, over and around big boulders. The going was much easier but the ice was very thin. We came to the canyon with sheer rock on either side: there was a bridge of ice on one side and white water on the other, leaping over the rocks. Allen tested the ice with an ax and got safely over, but it wasn't so easy with the dogs and toboggan. The ice slanted toward the open water and the toboggan would slide. He put a long rope on the bow and I held on to the tail rope...in this way we got everything and everyone across. As we neared the foot of the mountain the ice got more solid, but Tip would take no human's word for it and kept testing it with his paw before he'd lead his team across.

February 15, 1936. We continued on the stream when possible and along the bank when we found open water. Strange as it may seem we were running short on grub and dog food.

A caribou and a half does not last long with 10 ravenous dogs. We came to the White River and crossed to the opposite bank where it was open. There was one log across on which Allen crossed and cut poles to build a bridge. I sat on the toboggan and rested... I was coughing and had pain in my chest. It took an hour to get the dogteams across. It was noon and I suggested we have lunch. We could get clear water and have tea that tasted like tea and not like spruce boughs. I felt so weak I wondered how I could put one snowshoe in front of the other all afternoon. I thought it was due to the fact we'd only had coffee for breakfast. We hope to come to a trading post at Snag on the White River in two days.

Allen said "Maybe Jack Dolan no home. Sometime stay on trapline two months." It was a pleasant prospect to look forward to but we are supposed to be able to live off the country if we have to. There were fresh moose tracks and we hoped to be able to get one. Since breaking his own gun Allen has carried my 30-06 on his toboggan.

I felt much better after tea and we went on through the woods. The underbrush was very thick and the toboggan was catching on trees...but the dogs were going very fast. They smelled game. I had a hard time keeping up with them on snowshoes that were also catching on snags, and branches were slapping on my face. I fell down many times.

We hit the river again and took off our snowshoes. The dogs were wild with excitement, with the many tracks of moose to follow, and the going was very good on the river although we had to watch out for slush ice. We stopped at noon and had tea along the bank of the White. The whole White valley lay north and south with high mountains on either side, and what looked like a white mist in the dark sky was the sun going down. Allen again voiced his doubt about the possibility that Jack Dolan may not be home. Perhaps he wanted to prepare me for the worst; however I was in no mood to be prepared. A hungry woman is not to be trifled with, especially one with a pain in her chest. "He'd better be home or I'll break down his door." Allen looked quite shocked... an Indian of course would not dare break into a white man's cabin, but I was quite capable of it. Desperation makes for boldness. What's a trading post without a trader, and a trader's place is at his post.

We had hoped to find snowshoe tracks of some trapper but we came across no signs of human habitation, and we were very close to Snag. A coyote appeared and the dogs, who are always looking for some sign of game, took after it ...so we arrived long before we expected. There were three or four cabins, but no smoke and no sign of life. We went on a little farther and there was smoke curling up from a chimney. Allen rapped on the door and shouted back at me "Dolan Home." He had arrived two days before from Stewart, 400 miles away and it had taken him two months.

SNAG. TRADING POST OF JACK DOLAN YUKON TERRITORY

Jack Dolan came out and helped me to unharness the dogs. He was a little skinny man, much smaller that I am, with long brown hair down to his shoulders. A wide stiff brimmed brown hat sat strait on his head. He didn't walk...he seemed to glide and always to one side like a man that had followed a dogteam for many years. He had come here 25 years ago during the Chisana gold rush and had never married, not even an Indian. He would sit for hours with his head in his hands. I wondered vaguely what had brought him, and more strongly why he stayed. Life does not hold the same meaning for all...certainly he wasn't getting rich from the Indians. Very few of them were trapping and most of them were dying from tuberculosis, even the children. He seemed rather to belong to that group of men, lone prospectors who have from the early days written their names across the pages of Alaskan history. Though they have not found gold in a mine or a creek, they have found gold in the sunsets and through the years clutch hope tight to their breasts.

I was very curious to know how my guide would be accepted here among the Indians. Four years ago he had come with his dogteam and carried off the Chief's daughter to the lake of Kluane. She evidently had not pleased him for he returned her to the home of her father within the year. He said "she wouldn't talk", and I had thought silence a golden thing in a woman.

The Indians now came in and drawing chairs close to the fire, slumped down with a greeting to no one. For hours they sat slumped over like so many statues made of stone. They made me nervous. I asked Mr. Dolan why they sat there and he said "to keep warm so they don't have to chop wood for themselves." Jonny Allen now came in at dark. He didn't glance at his wife nor did she look up. It seemed impossible to me that they'd once held each other close and now have nothing to say to each other.

The second day a young white trapper came in. His Indian wife had died the year before. He spoke of her with sadness in his voice. He said "I'll see that Allen takes back his wife." And here was white man's law speaking with revenge. The Chief himself was over 60 and stood well over six feet. He was like a man already dead, his spirit seemed killed, no hope gleamed from his eyes. His daughter seemed willing to bear any burden that might be placed upon her shoulders...her love was giving even unto death...making no demands. They would all come to the trading post in the early morning, sit all day, and not utter a sound. It was very depressing,

I felt very ill myself and so weak I could hardly walk. I had the most severe pain in my chest and a lump in my throat where my Adam's apple should have been. I wondered if I were going to have pneumonia and die here in the wilderness. What would become of the dogs?

The first night we had arrived I had examined Allen's foot that had hurt him all the way from Kluane. I picked out with a tweezers a splinter an inch long which he had very carefully sealed in with "new skin" and adhesive so that it couldn't have come out had it wanted to. I had also asked Jack Dolan if he had any mustard, but he didn't.

The mentholatum I carried in my own medicine kit would not touch this something that seemed to be closing up my lungs, nor destroy the lump that stopped my breathing.

What a coward I am, but how lonely the wilderness. How far far away from anyone who cares whether I live or die, and people are dying from the "flu" this winter with the best of care. I am quite sure now I am going to die, but I should not mind so much if I had someone to hold my hand.

During the long nights I could hear Allen and Dolan snoring in the trading post. I could have gotten up and with my bare hands strangled both of these unconcerned men, there in their beds. I wondered if I got worse whether to send Allen back to Kluane to wire for a plane. But would they take the dogs, and I'd most likely be better or dead before a plane could get here.

There was nothing to do but wait and in the meantime try everything I could...I had so little with me...I had not planned on getting the flu but they had all had it at Kluane Lake before I'd gotten there. I could not eat, but drank huge amounts of caribou broth. Jack Dolan found a belladona plaster which I applied the second day, and hoped I may be able to leave the next.

The next morning however I was gasping for breath and couldn't speak above a whisper. The belladona had done no good. I got up in desperation. I must get out of here I thought, and I was very indignant. This was a trading post, store, and home. And none of them have mustard. I've never been in a home where they didn't have mustard. Perhaps if I got back on the trail I might feel better; anything was better than this.

I got dressed and went into the kitchen where they were having breakfast. "But you must have mustard...someplace...somewhere." Dolan said "well I used to have some around...you might find it in the store."

I started looking and finally found it behind a lot of boxes. He said "the lid has been off it for three years and it most likely isn't any good." I tasted it and it was quite like flour, but this is what I needed, an old fashioned remedy. When I finished mixing it. I ripped off the belladona and applied the mustard very carefully. It seemed nice and warm and seemed to give immediate relief. I went to bed and quickly fell asleep.

When I woke up I realized I would apply no more mustard plasters for many a day to come and would most likely carry the scars of this one to Fairbanks...but I felt much better and my chest was loose. There seemed to be nothing more I could do in the matter of first aid. If anything I had done too much and I might as well take off.

I packed in the evening but the next morning still felt very weak and decided to wait another day. Allen went hunting but returned in the evening with no game. Dolen cooked dog feed and I stayed in bed all day.

CHAPTER 9.

SNAG TO TANANA CROSSING

February 21-March 1, 1936. By the 21st of February we had been here in Snag four days. Allen's foot was better and although I was still very weak, my throat and chest were improved and I was really afraid to stay any longer as I did not want friends to think I was lost...but I was also afraid to leave. Dolan was going on his trap line as soon as we left so I asked him to wait two days so if I got worse I could come back.

We lashed the toboggans and hitched up the dogs. Tip was feeling quite frisky and took a bite at Stikine where upon all the brothers had him down in a minute. I thought they would tear him apart, and all I could do was scream. I can usually manage my own dogs but I could hardly help harness them this morning. Thankfully Jonny got them apart while a dozen Indians stood around openmouthed. It is always a miracle to me how Tip emerges from these skirmishes without a scratch, and as cocky as ever. The brothers wouldn't touch him if he didn't bother them. They will put up with his growls, but as soon as he bites one of them he has the rest of them to answer to.

We had 25 miles to go to the cabin of Chief Johnson, Allen's father-in-law, where we hoped to pick up dried meat for the dogs. Dolan could give us very little as he was short himself. We had a broken trail for two miles and then put on snowshoes, and what a snow. I had been told that there was always a light snowfall, and only on the coast did we get heavier snow. That's what they say in the interior. I do not mind breaking trail when my snowshoes only go down to my knees, but I do resent it when I go down up to my neck and the snow gets in my ears. Both of us went ahead of the dogs, and very slowly.

Around noon we heard another dogteam behind us and saw Indians coming. I thought to myself "isn't that just like the Indians to let us break trail, then come along behind." I wished I could pick up the trail after me, but they very shortly caught up with us. It was Chief Johnson himself and he went ahead of Allen. I was very much ashamed of myself, and Allen, who was tired from breaking trail all morning, dropped in behind me. We then changed the dogteams and put my team ahead. We continued this all afternoon, the three of us walking ahead and three dogteams following, with Mrs. Johnson bringing up the rear. We had to camp 10 miles this side of his cabin.

February 22, 1936. We made Chief Johnson's cabin at 11:30, had lunch and decided to leave the dogs here and break trail ahead. Allen and I broke trail all afternoon, returning at dark when we fed the dogs and ourselves. I was very tired and so was Allen.

February 23, 1936. We left at 9:00 A.M. and covered the trail that it took us so long the day before to break, in an hour and a half. Then deep, deep snow. We were all inside the cabin at noon, and felt much better after tea. We trudged along all afternoon, both of us going ahead of the dogs, and coming back to lift the toboggans out of the grass clumps. If the dogs stop they can't get the toboggans started again. My dogs look at me as if they think I'm crazy and there are times when I think they're right. Paws once lifted to my hands in salute now remain on the ground...eyes that once looked into mine with nothing but adoration now look with reproach.

About 3:00 in the afternoon we came to a lake, and the broken trail of the Scotty Creek Indians...there were three or four inches of snow on it, but it had a solid foundation.

Allen stopped his team, took off his snowshoes and jumped on the back of his toboggan. He looked around and said "blue sky coming up."

It was a dark gray day. I looked up into the heavens and told him "it's the broken trail you found rather than any blue in the sky."

We rode for a ways and then went ahead again so as to save the dogs as much as possible. Crossed the headwaters of little Scotty Creek, which flows down into the Tanana. There was much overflow on the ice and we had to put brush on it to keep the toboggans from getting wet. Followed Indian trail across two lakes until we hit Little Scotty again at 5 o'clock. There was deep water so we turned around and camped for the night. It was zero degrees and it seemed very hot.

February 24, 1936. It's 20 below this morning, the sun is shining and the barometer is rising...so we can look for colder weather. We hit Scotty Creek again. The dogs were going pretty fast when I heard ice cracking and saw it bend under Allen's team. We left the creek and hit the edge of a lake with glare ice. As we were rounding a bend, the toboggan started sliding and I jumped off to steady it and went right through the ice up to my waist. I screamed for Allen but my dogs had stopped and I was out of it long before Allen could reach me. It was a nuisance having to stop and build a fire. Everything froze immediately...

I even had to thaw out my socks before I could pull them off, and it wasn't too warm changing to corduroy pajama pants. I had sent my other ski suit to Fairbanks by plane, and now my toboggan was all iced down making it twice as heavy to pull for the poor dogs. We scraped off as much as possible. Very shortly after this we crossed the boundary line, 100 feet of slashed timber marking the boundary between the Yukon and the Territory of Alaska [statehood wasn't until 1959].

All afternoon we have been dropping down into the Tanana Valley. We came through scrub brush, creeks and lakes, but hit no more slush ice. I doubt if my sled could carry any more without sinking anyway. At 4:00 I had my first glimpse of the headwaters of the Tanana and the village of Scotty. There were a dozen buildings and it seemed gorgeous to see a cabin again. The place was deserted. I picked the largest and most beautiful log cabin to stop in, on the highest hill commanding a magnificent view of the river. I walked up to take possession. I felt as if I'd just as soon spend the rest of my life here. But it seemed that I wasn't going to spend it in this particular cabin...the door was locked and bolted. We went around to all the cabins and the smallest one was the only one unlocked.

We hoped to find the Indians here to get information about trading posts and food for the dogs, but they seemed to have left the country. We fed the dogs the last bit of dried meat we had...they have been going on half rations for a couple nights. We built a large fire and dried out the toboggans. On the door of one of the cabins is written "God, me good Indian....I want lynx, coyote, wolf, mink." It looked as if someone has promised him if he'd be good, all the good things of life would be his. After he's been a Christian a couple of years, he will begin to doubt that statement.

February 25, 1935. We very reluctantly left a warm cabin and followed an Indian trail down the river. There was no way of knowing how long since the Indians had been over it. It was covered with snow and at least a month old. We were grateful for any kind of a trail. Twenty five miles farther on we hoped to come to a trading post I had been told about before leaving Kluane.

All day we followed the trail, and about 3:00 we came to another deserted cabin and Allen pointed to the base of a mountain where a trading post is supposed to be. We kept on the trail until nearly dark when Allen thought the trail was going away from the post, perhaps to some trapping grounds of the Indians. We retraced our trail and came back to stay in the cabin all night. I climbed the ladder to the cache, but it was empty. We fed the dogs our emergency rations. Ten pounds of oatmeal for 10 starving dogs, and a thin slice of bear fat. They wagged their tails in appreciation, thinking this was just a little extra until they really got fed. When they saw that was all they were going to get, they howled in protest, and I closed my ears and went inside to warm up the last half inch of burned mulligan. I thought perhaps we should save this.

Allen thought the trail led in the wrong direction. I got out the compass and map. The trail seemed to lead to the north. I was so glad the lines on the map, the compass, and the trail all agreed, but it didn't really matter anyway... regardless of what any of them read we would have to follow the trail and just hope it would lead to human habitation and food. We couldn't very well break a fresh trail on empty stomachs, and the dogs needed a rest and lots of food. There were snowshoe tracks from this cabin also leading toward the west.

I looked around the cabin and found a note addressed to Maggie... romance on the Tanana. It was not sealed and I read it. "Maggie - I go Nabesna. Sorry I no see you."

So was I, very sorry I did not see him. Nabesna was just the place I wished to come in contact with. I got out the wire I had received two weeks before at Kluane and read "at Nabesna on the headwaters of the Tanana you will come to a trading post owned by a German...he is very hard to understand on account he can't wear his store teeth, but a very good egg. He will do everything possible to help you."

I could have cried. There is this good egg, I don't care if he has a hair on his head or a tooth in his mouth, just so his cache is full. I'm hungry. Where are the herds of caribou I was told would block my trail. There isn't even a wolf in this country, nothing for them to live on. I even thought back of the eight slices of bread I had so lavishly heaped on Chief Johnson and his poor wife. And so in my selfishness, fell asleep.

February 25, 1936. I had been so concerned about my stomach I had not noticed how cold it was getting. The thermometer registered 50 below when we got up at six and had coffee. I suggested to Allen he go take a look and see where the other snowshoe tracks went. He seemed to be gone a long time, but finally arrived with the news. "White man...over there, lots of food and smoked salmon for dogs. Nabesna...30 miles north."

We harnessed the dogs and arrived there in an hour. How good it was to see a white man again, especially one that could bake bread. It was actually the best bread I had ever tasted in all my life. I ate eight slices just to get even with Chief Johnson. We were the first people he had seen in two months, and I was the first white person in four months. He seemed almost as glad to see us as we were to see him. He climbed up to his cache and brought down smoked salmon from the lower Yukon, the first I had seen since leaving the Taku. We gave each of the dogs a whole salmon and then started a cooked feed for them in the evening.

I sat around all day and ate lots of bread...it tasted better than candy. In the north after baking a batch of bread the loaves are put outside to freeze, and brought in as needed and thawed out so that it always tastes like fresh bread. I asked him for the recipe, which he gave me in great detail with more pride that any cook I have ever known. I could not blame him. It was better bread than I had ever known. I'll give the recipe to you. I'm sure he wouldn't mind. I have since tried it myself and can recommend it. It should be good... it has all the rising properties I have ever heard of and some that I have not. This is NOT sourdough bread.

NABESNA BREAD

THREE STAR HOPS - put in tiny sack, 1 x 2 inches. Boil ½ hour. Squeeze.
3/4 cup rice
2 potatoes
1 cup sugar
1 tablespoon salt
1 teaspoon ginger cooked in 2 quarts water

½ cup flour, stirred in cold water. Add to the above mixture while still boiling, stir and boil, as in gravy. Cool. When luke warm add one yeast cake that has been dissolved in tepid water. Stir and when cool, put in quart jars. Add to these jars the quarts of fruit in your root house. It takes 3/4 cup of this conglomeration for eight loaves of bread, and is enough to last all winter. Don't forget to squeeze and be sure to take out the sack. [I would assume you add this to enough flour to make a whole lot of loaves.]

February 27, 1935. It was 50 below when we got up to leave but warmed up to 40 before we hit the trail. The old man decided to go with us and visit the town of Nabesna for a couple of days. It was fairly good going, but not good enough for all of us to ride. We were not out on the trail very long until I realized he was becoming very tired. At noon we stopped and had lunch. He asked me if anything was wrong with his nose and sure enough it was frozen. He thawed it out with snow and started on ahead of us. I asked Allen to give him a ride when he caught up with him and as Allen passed I heard him say "want ride", but there was nothing for him to hang onto. While I was running in front of my team that carried all the supplies, Allen, with his light load rode on ahead of us all in spite of my calling to him several times...I was indignant. The old man could not travel fast and he was very cold. I took off my scarf and tied it around his face. I caught up with Allen and told him if we left the old man alone he would most likely freeze to death. We started again, very late in the afternoon. I ran ahead of my team and the old man followed hanging on to the handlebars. Allen rode on far ahead of both of us. I had no great desire to ride but I was furious to be left alone and this was not the first time. I put on more speed, caught up with Allen, and jumped on his toboggan and stayed there til we crossed the Tanana to go into Nabesna, although I would have been more comfortable walking. It was too cold to ride but it slowed Allen down to our speed, so we all arrived together and intact. There is nothing more disheartening that to be left alone on a lonely trail far behind a dogteam.

I tied Tip and turned over the toboggan. There seemed to be many Indians around it but I caught no glimpse of a white man. We all went in and had tea with the Indians. It was 50 below and I wanted a warm cabin to stop in and warm food to eat if possible, and this is where the German trader was supposed to be. I was to learn our traveling companion and the trader were not on speaking terms, which was their business and not mine. I now spoke of going there when the old man spoke up and said "Oh no, we dasn't go there...him and me is bitter enemies." "Well maybe you dasn't but I dast"...and sent Allen down to find out. When he returned we drove our dogs down to the trading post, and the old man was staying with the Indians.

We unharnessed our team while the trader held a light. He then led the way into the most beautiful log cabin, and as he opened the door eight large white animals sprang up and surrounded us. I was frightened for a moment but when he spoke to them they all wagged their tails and here was the most magnificent dogteam I have ever seen. They all looked like big white wolves, but were friendly and came up to be petted.

He fed us and told me he was coming to meet me but got no information and thought perhaps I had gone a different route. He wanted me to stay over a day and rest, but as I had just rested a day and was long overdue, decided to leave the next morning. I brought in my sleeping bag and spread it on the floor but he'd have none of it. He fixed his own bed for me with clean sheets and a pillow and then put a large canvass around the whole thing, making a bedroom... then told me to take off my clothes and get a good rest.

I did... it was the first time I'd had them off since leaving Snag, and the first bed I'd slept in. I was deeply grateful.

February 28, 1936. He got up, got breakfast ready, and then called me. Is it any wonder I like to stop at trading posts. He kept up a continual flow of conversation, only part of which I could understand... but it didn't matter. Our traveling companion of the day before came in and bid me goodbye though neither of the men spoke to each other. It seemed quite funny but it was their affair, not mine, and I was not carrying the quarrels of men down the Tanana with me.

We harnessed the dogs and I wanted to pay for our food and lodging, but he wouldn't hear of it. He put on his fur cap and with his 8 dogs following, led us out of the town and put us on the right trail. It was a fairly good trail, but we were on the Tanana now where they use 22 inch sleds and drive their dogs double. Our dogs were driven tandem, and our toboggans were 16 inches wide. To keep the toboggan in the middle of the trail the dogs would have to walk between the runners where the snow had not been broken down. It was too much to expect from a dog, so they kept in the trail of one runner with the toboggan piling up the snow on one side. It was much better however than no trail.

We covered the 25 miles to Tetlin in five and a half hours, and arrived there just at dark. There were many log cabins but all of them seemed deserted...there was no smoke curling from the chimneys and that usually meant desertion. The cabins seemed sprawled over the whole side of a hill on both sides of the river, and were laid out in city blocks. I was not used to cities. I held the dogs on one side of the river while Allen went up the hill to find someone. He came back with a trader in tow, who helped me turn my team around and led me back to a large deserted building which turned out to be the hospital. The nurse was on her vacation and I was to stay in this large building by myself. I was not used to so much space. There were many beds... how did I choose one to sleep in. I thought I'd rather put my sleeping bag behind someone's stove. It had all been arranged however that when Mary Joyce came along with her dogteam she was to have the best in town afforded. I was deeply touched and deeply grateful. Why should these people trouble themselves about me and be so very kind.

It was as if I had been their wandering child come home. I was to learn the meaning of hospitality along the banks of the Tanana.

There was a fire started in the basement of the hospital and I was left to wash up while smoked salmon was brought for the dogs. The school teacher and his wife came down to see me. This was his first job, and they had just arrived the day before. They were both very young and very excited and very enthusiastic. They invited me for breakfast the next morning which unfortunately I couldn't make.

The trader came back and we went over to his cabin to eat. I asked why the town was so deserted and he said the Indians are out on their trap lines; they'll be back in March and all their children with them. School starts in April and lasts all summer until they go back trapping in the fall." It seemed like a good idea but hard to get used to.

February 29, 1936. This morning I was awakened and was told Joe Crosson [famous Alaskan bush pilot] was looking for me. The report had come over the radio the night before. I was very much ashamed...if I wished to go through the wilderness it was my own business, but I should see that I got there under my own power. There was no way of sending any report until I got to Tanana Crossing, and that would take two long days of traveling.

We harnessed the dogs and started at daybreak. The trader gave us two days smoked salmon as we wouldn't come to another trading post until we reached Tanana Crossing. He also sent his son with us for 10 miles to help break trail. Our own dogs were very tired.

We traveled as fast as we could all day, hoping to come to a shelter cabin that was located 30 miles from Tetlin. The snow was deep through the woods even on the broken trail, and in the open no trace of a trail at all... much time was lost in looking for it.

Allen had left his snowshoes behind at Nabesna. He had been told we'd have a broken trail all the way and so we did...but it had snowed six inches. Even with two inches of snow, once you have become used to snowshoes it's much easier walking with them. I went ahead and broke trail with my team following me. They did not wish another dogteam between us. Allen came along with his team, hanging on to the handlebars. The poor fellow was having a hard time of it, breaking through the crust with every other footstep. I'd just as soon leave one leg behind as a pair of snowshoes...one couldn't be much more helpless.

It took three hours going up Tetlin Summit, and it was getting dark when we reached the top. The trees were so heavily ladened with snow, not one green branch could be seen. They looked like grotesque snowmen. The wind was blowing on top of the mountain and here stretched below me was the whole Tanana valley. I don't think I have ever looked upon a more frightening scene or anything more desolate. I felt very small and understood for the first time why the pilots had warned me not to come this way. It stretched for miles and miles toward the north and south and seemed not so much one river, but a hundred different rivers flowing in all directions... some were frozen and some were running white water. It was a disturbing scene to gaze on and it put terror into my heart.

The wind and snow were biting my cheeks as we drove to the edge of the mountain and looked over. "Now don't tell me I have to go down the side of that thing?" It was almost two miles straight up and down. I had not come this far without going up and down a few mountains, but they were usually winding trails. One tipped the toboggan on its side, put one foot on the brake and held the sled with the weight of your body and hopped along on the other foot. If you lost your balance your sled tipped over and down the mountain. It was a thing to be avoided at all costs. It entailed a lot of work, and might break a dog's leg to say nothing of your own neck if you happened to hit a tree.

None of this seemed to bother Jonny Allen...he seemed more like a part of his dogteam, although he did get the splinter in his foot trying to stop the toboggan with his foot instead of a brake. I had a good mind to tell him now if he got another splinter in any part of his anatomy I would not take it out. I got out two dog chains and put a lock brake abound the box of my toboggan. Allen started down first with no brakes and the last I saw of him, before I had to turn my attention to my own team, he was hanging on to his tail ropes and was himself being pulled along on his fanny with his two legs stuck out in front of him, bracing himself.

I stepped on my brake, which wasn't much good in loose snow, swung low, and the dogs galloped down the mountain. You'd be passed a tree before you even saw it. It was fun.

We decided we couldn't make the shelter cabin, as it was too dark to find the trail, so got out the rag house for the night and then found we had left our caribou steaks on the rooftop of the trading post at Nabesna. It came down to rice and beans... what did it matter; tomorrow we get to Tanana Crossing. How I hoped I might get there before Joe Crosson, so I could go into Fairbanks with him for the Ice Carnival. I was now too late to make it by dogteam. We left early in the morning, a fog hung low and thick. I went ahead breaking trail with my team following me.

About 10:00 we came to the cabin and Allen went in to look around. We instantly noticed a pair of snowshoes, debating whether to take them or not. We decided it would be alright as whoever they belonged to would be ahead of him on the trail or else at Tanana Crossing. Allen now went ahead. We stopped at one o'clock to build a fire and make tea when suddenly we heard the roar of a plane. "But no pilot would be out in this fog, that can't be Joe Crosson... it must not be." Up and down, up and down the Tanana it flew... we couldn't see it, we could only hear it. I found myself screaming directions at him as if he could hear me, or as if I knew his business better than he knew it himself. When it seemed as if he were going to take off our very heads, I grabbed two burning sticks and waved them at him. I don't know how I expected him to see us when we couldn't see him. As if in answer to my prayer, the plane headed north toward Tanana. But one does not have planes looking for one if they can help it and if anything happened to Alaska's beloved Joe Crosson one might just as well go into the wilderness and stay there. I wondered if we'd be able to reach Tanana tonight, perhaps with empty sleds. We were going very slowly, the dogs were tired and we lost much time looking for the trail. The wind had blown away all traces of a dogteam or sled ever having been over it.

But I was determined to get word to Fairbanks tonight. "We'll leave our loads here and come back tomorrow for them." I don't know what the guide thought of this, but I ripped the load off my toboggan and covered it with canvass, and he did the same. We started on and traveled all afternoon. The sun went down... it had gone down in my heart long before. We were going through tundra with a scrub brush here and there, no trees... the Tanana River lay to our right but where was Tanana Crossing? I had not known it could be so far. There were no words spoken between us. We saved our energy to encourage the dogs who now could hardly pull empty sleds. Perhaps they had lost faith in us. The wind started to blow and it got dark.

We went on and on with our heads down, the dogs following and despair in my heart. It was a blizzard by this time. I had heard of men freezing to death outside their cabin door. Was I to be so close to Tanana Crossing and never get there. But we had to get there... we had left our sleeping bags back on the trail.

I had been told we would come to a landing field first and by that we would know we were close to Tanana Crossing. I have been looking for this field for hours and wondered now if we left the sleds, would we get there any faster? I began to think if it were much farther, the dogs would be pulling me instead of an empty toboggan.

We finally came to a patch of land where there wasn't even any scrub and in the middle of it are tracks from the skis of an airplane. That object there in the dark must be a plane, but perhaps we'd better go up to make sure. "I'm so glad they left a plane or I shouldn't have recognized the field!"

TANANA CROSSING

Have you ever been out in some isolated spot where you haven't had mail for months? Have you ever lived on a frozen river without seeing another woman for six months? I have, and when you get one letter it's as if Santa Claus had arrived... and when you dance it's as if you were dancing into the very gates of heaven. If you have never known any of these things, then you will never know how glad I was to get to Tanana Crossing. I did not know for sure I'd ever get there until I actually arrived...but that's what made it exciting.

We drove our teams up to the Pacific Alaska Airways station, and before we could stop, the operator and his wife were out to meet us. I kissed them both and could have cried in their arms but it would have looked so silly. She said she had been so afraid they'd persuade me to go by way of Dawson because they had wanted to see me. How badly I've wanted to see them... for 20 days.

All the dogs in the village started to howl. They smelled strange dogteams and from across the river every door was opened and Indians poured forth and came running over and into the station. It was a hard task getting them out but I was so hungry. We had dinner and I went in search of smoked salmon for the dogs. Now when I took a good look at them, they seemed pathetically thin, and Nakinaw was chewing on an old bear skin we had given him for a bed.

Joe Crosson had gone two days before. How was I to know he had followed my trail from the sky all the way from Kluane Lake... and after losing it there, had landed on the lake where they told him I had gone on that morning. And a wire from Walter Hall, "Tell Mary Joyce I have her other pair of pants, got them from Bob Randall at

Whitehorse, and for her to put on a little more speed." Wires from Juneau, Taku, Whitehorse, Kluane Lake, and Fairbanks. Never mind what was in them...I'm not going to tell. How good it was to hear from the outside world again.

There was to be a dance tonight...any occasion was an excuse for a dance. At every Indian camp I have stopped at there has been a victrola and their favorite records are "The Isle of Capri" and "She'll Be Coming Round the Mountain". I forgot I was tired. The Indian boys were dressed in white shirts and ties, good looking riding breeches and knee-length beaded moccasins. The girls wore bright colored dresses and were very pretty. When the boys asked the girls to dance they would come up and bow, from the hip down, with their hand on their chest, elbow out. King Arthur himself couldn't have been more chivalrous. The boys were very good dancers. They didn't know the latest steps, neither did I, but they seemed to possess the music and their bodies swayed to its rhythm. I noticed my guide giving some of the girls the "come hither" look and they would giggle. He seemed to be the guest of honor, after all he had come with the white lady from the lake of Kluane. He didn't seem to be doing so badly...perhaps that's why it took him weeks to get home afterwards.

I stayed at Tanana Crossing four days with the Okerlands, the operator and his wife. There were no planes as a low thick fog hung over the whole Tanana Valley, from here to Fairbanks. The first day I had a message from Robie saying "Will be after you in the morning if OK by you." And how it would be OK by me.

The Ice Carnival at Fairbanks started the fifth of March and I had been made [1936] Miss Juneau by the Chamber of Commerce. You see when you're in the wilderness you have no control over what they make you. There had been no contest, no one else had a chance, I was merely appointed because I was going anyway. I would not lead you astray into thinking I am beautiful.

Here I met the man who ran all the trading posts where I had been receiving so much kindness... (with the exception of the post at Nabesna which was owned by the German). He was a tall dark handsome man, dark hair and eyes, humorous mouth, and I do not believe I have ever seen so much tolerance in the face of any man. Perhaps he needed tolerance.

There is a missionary here and a school to bring white man's civilization to the savages. If they are savages, we are barbarians. They got along much better before we ever came, and how can we be so sure we are bringing to them something that is better than theirs. We are very conceited to think we can bring God to a people that already possess Him. We come in the name of God and if we care to be honest even to ourselves, we came to fill our own pocketbooks. We who claim to be so civilized, by what standards do we measure our own civilization. The world war to end all wars perhaps. If we must be barbarians then let us not be barbarians in the name of Jesus Christ. There are already too many crimes committed in His name.

A trader and a missionary are never on speaking terms. Why should they be? The trader came to trade. He admits it. The missionary came to bring the gospel, but the Indian girls, after learning to write, convert their bibles to Sears and Roebuck and Montgomery Ward catalogues "so they can buy lipstick and pretty clothes to make themselves beautiful so Indian boys marry them in white man's churches." Or maybe a few will marry a white man. Their demands are getting modern. "Johnny, when you go to Fairbanks bring me shoes...high heel shoes." And Johnny most likely will. They sit at a counter and say "ice cream, chocolate taste."

Emma came in one night. She was gloriously tight and woe be the white man who gave her the makings. She put her head back and shrieked with laughter. Emma should be dignified. It is only a few days until her wedding. The bride's gown is already here from Sears and Roebuck. Emma has been married a couple years but she's a Christian now and civilized. Johnny shall be made to do right by her. Johnny isn't so sure, he doesn't see why he should be made to marry her twice, and he doesn't like church weddings anyway.

Perhaps he has no pretty clothes. It wasn't long until Emma didn't feel quite so good. There were groans now where there had been laughter, and the words that flowed from her mouth were not exactly the words of a prayer.

We put her on a cot. There was a knock on the door and the missionary entered. Silence reigned. He walked over and stood looking down on her face while she clasped his hand kissing it and said "Jesus Christ, Jesus Christ, Jesus Christ". I have never seen a man so bowed down by grief. His face was the picture of despair and the burden of it seemed more than he could bear.

The Northern Lights have seen strange sights, but I think the strangest they ever saw at Tanana Crossing was that night we bundled up Emma, laid her in my toboggan and with one missionary, one radio operator and one dog musher, we pulled her and pushed her across the Tanana and it was no easy task getting her up the bank on the other side. I remembered the story of the Marshall that had gone in to bring out a crazy man, how he had broken trail for days ahead of his dogs, starving himself and feeding the man lashed to his sled. How one night he finally reached a roadhouse, stumbling and falling down, willing hands assisted him... and the man on the sled sat up and said "who's crazy?"

The fifth day a plane arrived from Fairbanks. I had planned on leaving the dogs here and coming back for them after the carnival. The surrounding country looked even more desolate and unfriendly from the sky than it did on the trail, perhaps because one could see so much more of it. We flew over the trail to Fairbanks I would be taking with the dogs after the carnival. How small the cabins looked from above, but I know them to be mansions because I've been there. We saw several moose and a small herd of buffalo which we circled...they did not look very friendly. I am told they sometimes block the Richardson highway road.

Site of Fairbanks Ice Carnival
Beauty Contest, 1936

CHAPTER 10.

FAIRBANKS

March 5, 1936. Fairbanks, Golden City of the North, Home of the Pacific Alaska Airways. All things end at Fairbanks and from here all things begin. It is the end of the Alaska Railroad that has its beginning at Stewart. It is the end of the Richardson Highway that begins at Valdez. It is too vitally alive to say it "nestles" among the hills in a low rolling country - I'd say rather that it perched proudly on the banks of the Tanana, ready to strike back at any attempt to destroy it. Log cabins mingle with modern buildings that house a population of 6,000, in whose veins runs blood thick and red and fast. It mothers and serves the whole of the Interior of Alaska.

We swooped down on it and there was the Mayor, the Carnival Committee and all my friends to greet me; how good it was to see them all again. The Fairbanks Ice Carnival starts tonight with the selection of Miss Alaska, and would I enter the beauty contest? Not if I could help it. The girls were to parade in evening dresses, ski suits, and bathing suits. My clothes had not arrived from Juneau by plane, and anyway, I should show the legs that mushed a thousand miles?

For a week dogteams have been arriving from Indian villages on the lower Yukon, Nulato, Ruby, Kokrines, from Circle, north of

Fairbanks, from all the small villages around Fairbanks. A doctor brought his team from Nome by plane. Some arrived under their own power and others were brought by train. Siberians, Malamutes, Huskies and Wolf dogs, all to enter the Grand Dog Derby. Their howls all night mingled with gay laughter of a people who had cast all care aside, the long winter was over, spring was near, and the ice would soon go out. For two days people have been coming by plane from Nome, Nulato, Ruby, McGrath in the Northwest; 200 strong from Anchorage in the South by railroad; and many from Dawson by plane.

Hockey games and curling games, dances that lasted all night - Fairbanks never slept. They'd had the whole black winter to sleep in, and weeks to recuperate. The parade lasted all one afternoon with floats that could rival the Tournament of Roses...minus the roses.

The queen, Miss Alaska, was crowned down on the river where a throne had been built out of solid ice, 60 feet long and 40 feet high. The background was painted the most heavenly blue - they told me out of cake frosting. Icy steps led up to it with a painted red carpet in the middle. At the sides were tall Totem poles, crafted from clear blocks of ice, the work of an artist, and perhaps the most unique throne a queen has ever sat upon.

Thirty floats passed under the Fairbanks bridge...the Judge's Box and the Pacific Alaska Airways entry ran off with the honors. Johnny Allen (not my guide) won the dog races.

Here I joined the festivities for ten days before returning to Tanana Crossing to collect my dogs and finish my 1,000 mile trek by dogteam to Fairbanks.

CHAPTER 11.

TANANA CROSSING TO FAIRBANKS

March 16-25, 1936. My arrival back in Tanana Crossing was greeted by wild howls on the part of the dogs. I had to go over and pet each one separately, and they all talked to me and told me what a swell time they'd had and how well they'd been fed. They were all plump and peppy and their black glossy coats gleamed in the sunlight as their paws came up on my shoulders.

For the third time I asked the guide what he wanted to eat on the trail and for the third time I received the same reply "Me don't like white man's grub". I have found out myself I can travel much better on rice, beans and boiled meat than on anything else, with lots of fat. How disgusting. But that does not mean that I object to some of the delicacies, and when I take marmalade, the guide eats as much of it as I do.

Every young Indian in Tanana Crossing wanted to guide me as far as Big Delta...one wanted to go clear to Fairbanks. He said he had no dogteam, but would walk, he wanted a divorce. Civilization brings complications. I picked the one that talked the least - Tim. I do not like my landscapes cluttered up with a lot of jabbering.

We left the P.A.A. radio station on a beautiful Spring morning. This is what every dog musher dreams of...spring, blue skies, and a hard trail. The whole town turned out to see us off as we headed our teams down the valley.

At noon we stopped to rest ourselves and the dogs. Now instead of building a fire to make tea we drank coffee out of a thermos bottle.

There is perhaps a vast difference between the people of British Columbia and the people of the Yukon. But the only difference I have noticed between Yukoners and Alaskans is that one drinks tea and the other drinks coffee.

We reached the top of the hill and Tim stopped his team ahead of me. There he stood outlined sharply against a flaming sky, tall and slender with his hand pointing to the sun going down in the West. This was so much a part of him I could not help but envy him and all his race. Sorrow followed envy. As the sun dies in the West, so dies the soul of his race.

We had a long and steep hill to go down. He said "You wait here and after I take my team down, I will come back for yours." I told him I could get down all right but he was afraid of it, that I would have a hard time holding back the dogs. He started down and my team followed. When he reached bottom he seemed surprised that I was behind him and in one piece.

That evening we reached an Indian camp and he told all the Indians about the steep descent I had come down...he kept repeating "My God, that steep hill you come down!" I had gained his respect. The trader from Tanana Crossing was there with his dogteam on his way back from Fairbanks with a brother of my guide. His dogs looked like big black wolves. They did not wag their tails and I was afraid of them. He told me if they ever get loose he has to set snares to catch them.

March 17, 1936. We all left the next morning early. Two dogteams for Tanana and two for Fairbanks. The second day was much like the first except I wished I had a 22 inch sled instead of a toboggan, however one can't change sleds for every locality. We again stopped at an Indian settlement for the night. I had a small cabin to myself, the door was closed and I was getting supper. I thought I was alone and when I turned around there were two Indian women sitting inside the door. I had not heard them come in nor did they speak until I discovered them...they started to giggle. But they had come for a purpose to tell me of their troubles. It seemed the Doctor at Fairbanks had not been down for a year and their stomachs hurt. "You give us medicine for stomach?" "But I have no medicine with me." And they went into detail about where it hurt and how and always ended up insisting I give them "medicine for stomach." I did not know how I would get rid of them. I didn't even have an aspirin to rid myself of them. I finally told them I would ask the Doctor in Fairbanks when I got there.

March 18, 1936. Another Indian accompanied us this morning who wanted to go to Healy, our next stop 33 miles distant. We wasted as little time as possible all day and traveled as fast as we could, even then it was dark when we hit Healy Lake, a wind was blowing and it seemed very cold. The Indians could see us coming across the lake and were all out to meet us. We had to go up a steep bank which was very slippery. I was the last, and just when I was near the top I lost my grip on the handlebars and went tumbling down again and the dogs went on without me. I was very much embarrassed and all the Indians laughed. It wasn't an easy task to climb up that slope with nothing to hang on to. When I finally did get up, the Indians came and shook hands with me. There must have been 30, some with babies on their backs. They turned that I might shake hands with the babies too. Now they were very solemn and dignified. They shook their heads and said "My, you come long way...we look for you, long time." How nice it is to have the Indians look forward to one's coming. We unharnessed the dogs and had tea. I had noticed two little girls raising a lot of dust in one of the cabins with brooms that were larger than they were. Shortly I was shown to this cabin.

March 19, 1936. I got up at six o'clock and cooked breakfast. We started out again, traveling on the winter trail down the Tanana. At ten we came to a cabin where two white men were trapping. They were waiting for us, and wanted to send mail to Fairbanks. They had just finished breakfast, and asked us to have some. I said "just coffee" but relented and ate a very large meal. I apologized for the amount, and they smiled. I'm sure they had never seen a woman eat so much before.

Every morning we'd get directions to the next cabin, the number of miles, and what to look for on the way. We were now supposed to come to Clearwater, the cabin of a white man by the bridge. At three o'clock we came to where a trail branched off to the left...this must be it. However after leading our dogs in we found it wasn't, although the water was clear and there was a bridge over it. We went on and on and finally came to it at dark. The river here stays open all winter and the trapper had fresh fish.

All along the way I have stopped at the cabins of trappers and prospectors where they were available. They are always glad to see some one, their doors are always open and what they have is yours...but I have never yet heard one of them speak of loneliness. Some of them don't see another man for months at a time and they never see a woman. One of them told me he was married and his wife was "outside". He wanted her to come back, and she wanted him to come out. She said "I never want to see that Godforsaken country again...wasting your life up here when you could have a good position down below." He said "yes, a white collar job, sitting at a desk all day: I didn't marry a desk, I married a woman and by God she'll live up here or else". Perhaps some day again America will breed a generation of women like our grandmothers, who could follow their men across the prairie in a covered wagon.

And that is why up here there are so many white men married to squaws because white women will not live outside of towns. It might not be too bad, especially if one could marry a man "with fast dog team". I know men in Alaska who are looking for Rex Beach and women who are looking for Dr. Grueling because the men once read a romantic story of the North by Beach, and Dr, Grueling told them there were ten men in Alaska to every woman and they can't find them.

Why look down on the white men married to squaws? Are they to blame because there are no more women who will pick up their skirts from around their dainty ankles and take a hike up Chilkoot Pass.....you figure it out, I gotta go to Fairbanks, but before I do let me tell you about one man's attempt to find a wife. Some of the men in isolated districts have used the mail order houses. I met one of them in Atlin. He wanted to give me ten dollars on account of I might need it before I got to Fairbanks. He had carried on correspondence with a woman down below. He wooed her by letters and finally won her. They usually exchange pictures so they have some idea what to expect and will recognize each other when she gets off the boat. This must have been dispersed with because when she landed at Atlin someone pointed him out to her and she threw up her hands in horror. I swear he didn't have a tooth in his mouth nor a hair on his head. It was not that he was so old, he just looked so weatherbeaten, like an old scarecrow blown by the wind. She remained to marry someone else and he got tight as a tick and took his bicycle at midnight and went back to his diggings. He told me this with tears in his eyes - it is the big sorrow of his life. He did say her husband later returned the fare he had sent her. But he can't forget it, it is always before him, especially when he is in his cups.

Another big Swede sent clear to Norway for his bride, though why Norway I don't know, because all the Swedes and Norwegians I know fight like cats and dogs. Two days before she got there his comrades got him drunk and kept him in a stupor in his cabin. They met the boat and when she got off, they took her up to his cabin where they had already put another lady in bed with him. She fled thinking he had come upon evil ways since coming to this North country. That's a pal for you. It was some time before he even found out what the trouble was, but he fixed it all...they said he was a good talker.

March 20, 1936. After a hearty breakfast we left the next morning and arrived at Big Delta or McCarty at 11:00 A.M.. This is a hotel on the Richardson Highway and run by Rika Whalen.

There was not even a white man here, so it is not men alone that seek the wilderness. It is around here that the buffalo roam and some of them with her cattle.

I put in a call to Fairbanks and was told the Grand Curlers Ball was that evening and would I please hurry, or should they hitch up all the stray dogs in town and come out and get me. It was only a hundred miles and they were already starting. But as long as there's one plane in Alaska I doubt I'll see the chechakos behind a dog team.

We left, of course after being fed. We were now supposed to travel on the left hand bank of the Tanana for five miles..the right was open running water. There was one final bridge of ice we could cross on the right bank and that was all that was needed to get up onto the Richardson Highway. Before that were three streams we had to cross which meant unpacking everything on the sleds, carrying it across, and repacking. Three times we had to do this... it took much time but when we did get started we made up for it. Too much so. The going was so good we must have gone ten miles, and missing our cutoff had to retrace our tracks. We found the bridge coming back and crossed to the Richardson. It was dark but we were making good time. Rabbits darted across the road and the dogs took after them. We arrived at a white man's cabin at 8:00. He had been looking for us but given up and eaten alone. He now put a big caribou roast in the oven to heat and placed our dessert on the table, large dishes of fruit. I was so hungry I ate the dessert first. Tim had better manners or perhaps he was bashful. We talked and laughed and then to bed.

March 21, 1936. From here the guide was going back and I was going on alone. There would be no more rivers to cross. The white man told me I'd had such a nightmare the night before and seemed in such distress that he almost awakened me. He said "you were mushing dogs". Well after all that, it's enough to give anyone a nightmare Perhaps I was hurrying to the Curler's Ball.

The guide started back to Tanana Crossing and the white man walked to the top of the hill with me. He noted the trail's drifted. The road was cut in the side of a mountain and at its edge was a sheer drop of 500 feet, with the open Tanana below. The snow had drifted on the mountain side and sloped toward the bank. My toboggan kept sliding toward it. We said goodbye at the top of the hill.

At noon I came to Richardson where there is a post office. Many come here by dogteam to get their mail. There are four or five cabins and one very large log hotel at the top of the hill, deserted. The roadhouses along the Richardson Highway did a flourishing business until the railroad was built, and what a railroad.

I've been on that railroad. I lay down on the seat and tried to sleep and nearly lost my head while doing it - such banging and clanging I've never heard before. One car would jump to the right while the other jumped to the left. It seemed they would jump right off the tracks. They didn't that time, maybe they waited for the next. It takes "brave men and bold" to run the Alaska Railroad.

But let's get back to the Richardson Highway, we are about to have lunch with a very charming gentleman, the postmaster of Richardson. I am at a disadvantage here because I can't surprise anyone since there is a telephone from roadhouse to roadhouse. It's really to my advantage as they always have food waiting for me. I'm afraid they have been discussing my appetite over it because there was a banquet set before me. I praised the food and ate and ate. He would urge me to have more, saying "perhaps you don't like it?" "But it was delicious." "But you didn't eat anything." "I couldn't possibly eat any more." "Oh well, I guess you don't like my cooking." I had already eaten enough for two men and used up all my adjectives in praising it.

It was one o'clock, the next roadhouse was 12 miles away, and I was lazy after so big a meal. The wind was blowing and I was afraid to go on but I was more afraid to stay for fear he'd kill me with his food. "She died from overeating." The telephone rang and it was the fox farm and the aunt of one of my best friends. "Is Mary Joyce there?" I hastened to answer it. "Betty has told me so much about you...are you coming on tonight?" I explained I would but I'm afraid it will be dark before I get there, my dogs are tired, and I'm not traveling very fast. I talked with her husband who told me to come along and he would meet me at Birch Lake. I left and I don't know to this day if the postmaster was serious or making fun of me. He may have thought me a glutton, and if he did he was quite right.

I had to practically drag the dogs away from that cabin, they thought they'd just as soon stay there as any place. There was a long hill to go up and I thought I'd never get to the top. They would look back at the cabin and give me dirty looks. After I got them out of sight, they were much better. One could see the gravel after the toboggan had been over the road. When I got lower the snow was deeper and I put on snowshoes and went ahead of the dogs. At six o'clock I saw another dogteam coming down the road. I had not quite gotten to Birch Lake.

He waved at me and drove his dogteam up to mine. I dashed out to hold Tip and pull my team off the trail saying "my dogs will fight." I am always scared to death to meet another team on the trail. He said they wouldn't fight his dogs and so they didn't. He took all my load and put it on his sled and we started out again. It did not take long to reach the lake and he shouted back to me "do you ever swear at your dogs?" He was a gentleman, he did not wait for an answer but said "You have to cuss em to mush em." He took many shortcuts I would not have known and most likely would have been lost in the dark. His wife had supper waiting for us. I felt I had known these people all my life.

March 22-23, 1936. I stayed here for two days. It was a very comfortable place. The wind was blowing, we heard over the telephone one car had started out from Fairbanks on the Richardson Highway and got snowed under before it could get out of town. It seemed almost impossible to me... they said "the wind is blowing 35mph in Fairbanks." That did not seem very fast to me, I come from country where it blows 95 miles an hour. The Taku wind is famous all over Alaska and very much dreaded. If you don't believe me read what Sherwood Wirt says about it in his "Cracked Ice" poem:

TAKU

If a zyphyr sends your hat
All the way to Sundum Flat-
That's no Taku wind

If the light poles in the street
Crash in splinters at your feet-
That's no Taku wind.

But if your garage
Backs out of your car-
If your suspenders
Give up with a yank-
If chunks of paving
Knock mountains ajar-
If you can't find
The First National Bank-

Stranger, that's a Taku wind.

March 24, 1936. We left this morning at eight o'clock. I had 33 miles to go to the next roadhouse. The fox farmer took my load for ten miles to a mink farm where we had lunch. Then the mink farmer took it for another ten miles. They both shot rabbits along the way for their mink and foxes...my dogs thought this was great sport. In the middle of the afternoon the mink farmer turned his team around, gave me my load, and went back to feed his mink. I now had only 13 miles to go to the next roadhouse. At four o'clock

I came to a cabin. The man and his wife were out by the road, and nothing would do but I go in and have tea with them. This was not hard work. We visited for an hour and I went on, arriving at "Eighteen Mile" roadhouse at 7:00 p.m.. The woman here was alone...it was her husband who had tried to get home in his car and was drifted in at Fairbanks. The highway is not kept open during the winter months. She fed me and we had a grand time visiting. She showed me pictures of the Harding party when they were there, when the late President visited Alaska.

And that is the Tanana River and the Richardson Highway. If I never again meet such grand people, I have met more than most people meet in a lifetime. There is something about it, something everyone gave me along the way that can't be bought and paid for... that no one else can give me. It is called "hospitality" for want of a better name, but part of the heart goes with it.

Mary Joyce and her Dogteam on Richardson Highway, Fairbanks.

CHAPTER 12.

FAIRBANKS...AGAIN

March 25, 1936. I did not leave this morning until ten o'clock. This would be my last day on the trail. I hated to have it over with. I perhaps will never again experience anything like it or possess so much happiness. I had 18 miles to go, it seemed so short a time until I was coming into the outskirts of Fairbanks, as if the dogs sensed the end of their journey and hurried toward it. There was the Pacific Alaska Airways truck coming to meet me and all my friends in it. We stopped and talked... there was much laughter and much wagging of dogs' tails. They all seemed surprised to see the dogs in such good condition, but then they had not seen them when I arrived at Tanana Crossing when they were almost eating their harnesses.

We looked up and saw a little short man coming down the road in a heavy coonskin coat. He came up to me and said "Aren't you coming into Fairbanks?" He looked quite hot and quite cross. I didn't know what he meant. He couldn't think I was going to turn around and go back the way I came, especially the same day. He waved his hand toward the Richardson Highway sign and said "the Committee awaits". There were a lot of people, I was embarrassed. I had expected my friends to meet me but I hadn't expected a committee. "Would they mind waiting one more minute until I powder my nose? One can't meet a Committee with a shiny nose."

I drove on to the sign and felt quite silly and the dogs didn't know what to make of it. They had never seen cars before and they were afraid of crowds. I finally got them quieted down and here I delivered a letter from our beloved Governor to the Mayor of Fairbanks, and received a lovely silver cup in return. It was more than I deserved, both the cup and the reception. The Mayor had been married only a few months. Many get the chance to kiss the bride, but I got a chance to kiss the bridegroom and the whole Carnival Committee...not bad.

They suggested I drive down the main street but how would I ever get the dogs through town? Tip followed the P.A.A. truck with his head up and tail curled and disdained to even look at another dog until we passed Joe Crosson's house. His little wire haired terrier crossed the street with a bone in his mouth. Tip whirled his team around in the middle of the street and started after him. I thought this deep ingratitude to a man who had looked for him on the trail. Joe came out and carried his little dog into the house. Another big wolf dog darted out from a house and I grabbed a snowshoe and one of the boys in the truck grabbed a crank. I shouted "don't kill him... I meant to only daze him."

We drove on to the dog pound and there the keeper of the pound told me Tip was the only good dog I had. In Alaska you may run down anything a man possesses, even his wife, and he will pay no attention to you. Run down his dogteam and you have a fight on your hands. It would do me no good to strike the man, perhaps only tickling him and making him as mad as a 22 does a bear...besides it made no difference to me what anyone thought of my dogs. They suit me and have followed me from Taku to Fairbanks, or I followed them, and they've worn out three dogteams. Anyway, I liked the man and anything he could say would make no difference today.

They had all waited to have lunch with me, and a jolly lunch it was. During the winter months in Fairbanks the women wear good looking ski suits on the street, swanky mukluks from Nome, and jaunty caps if they wear anything on their heads at all, and white or brown fur parkas. When they go to dances they don dinner dresses from New York but their husbands pockets are always bulging with mukluks, socks and bloomers that they'd worn there.

Fairbanks has perhaps the most unique telephone system in existence. If there is a fire any place all the women dash to the phone on the wall, take down the receiver and wait their turn to be told where it is. If the baby is asleep and they wish to go visiting, they call the operator, tell her where they are going, and leave the receiver down. When the baby wakes up and starts to cry, she calls them. If you're looking for a friend the operator can tell you she's at Mrs. So and So's home playing bridge. And if you're looking for your husband there are ten chances to one she'll know where he is although she may not always tell you this. Just one large happy family.

I went to see the doctor, a man who had lived in the country for many years. I still had a pain in my chest and thought perhaps I'd frosted my lungs in the fifty below temperatures on the trail. I also wanted to ask him about the Indian women with the pains in their stomachs. He and his wife were charming people, and I forgot both the pain in my chest and the women's stomachs, and walked off with an etching done by Ahgupuk, the Eskimo artist, instead of prescriptions.

All the old-timers stopped me on the street to say "I want to shake hands with the girl who drove her dogteam from Taku to Fairbanks."

And it was I who was honored, not they. Most of them had come into the country in the early days. Pioneers...they did me the honor of making me one of them. Let the Fairbanks News Miner tell you of it:

FAIRBANKS NEWS MINER, MARCH 25, 1936.

___Mary Joyce Ends Historic Journey__.

Bronzed by blazing spring sun reflected from measureless realms of snow, tanned by winds and weather of all sorts, yet with light heart and buoyant step, Mary Joyce, courageous woman musher, made her triumphant entry into Fairbanks this afternoon - completing a journey of some one thousand miles by dogteam and hanging up a record seldom if ever seen before reached in woman's world of achievement.

Neatly attired in dark blue hiking trousers, heavy blue woolen jacket, snug fitting black fur cap and knee length moccasins, Mary presented a striking picture as she swung down the homestretch and under the great sign marking the end of the Richardson Highway...

Met at the outskirts of the city by Mayor Collins..... and scores of private citizens, Mary was extended a splendid welcome...with her team of five beautiful dark-cast huskies....

–Mary Joyce to Enter Pioneer Women's Lodge-

Mary Joyce, famed Juneau woman dog musher, is to be admitted as an honorary member to the Fairbanks lodge of the Pioneer Women of Alaska at a special meeting of the lodge called for this purpose.... The late President's wife, Mrs. Florence King Harding, is the only other honorary member....etc.

I will never forget the people of Fairbanks.

Fairbanks Airport...Mary Joyce with Joe Crosson.

CHAPTER 13.

HOME

March 31, 1936. We left Fairbanks for the airport in the Pacific Alaska Airways large Ford with 9 people and eight dogs...two belonged to a prospector, my own five, and a beautiful little Siberian Malamute pup that Don Abel from Juneau had given me. My dogs are very much afraid of planes, especially when the engines roar and we start off. I had Tip in front with me so he wouldn't fight with his brothers. I went forward to sit down and there was Tip, sitting in my seat. He was too big to sit on my lap, and I couldn't sit on his. He sat there on the front seat as if he were president of the whole world, occasionally looking out the window and down on the ground. I think he thought this was much better than walking.

We landed at Kluane Lake and the guide Jonny Allen had not returned, but then I didn't think he'd be in any hurry...too many pretty girls along the way. This time when we left it was no trouble getting the dogs in the plane. They jumped in as if they were afraid they might get left behind.

It seemed remarkable to me, at this altitude we could see our dogteam trail. It looked as wide as a wagon road. I had thought that if we were lost no one could ever find us. We saw a lonely dogteam driver at the end of the lake and I understood for a moment why pilots look down on dog mushers. We landed at Whitehorse and stayed there for the night.

April 1, 1936. The P.A.A. plane went back to Fairbanks and we came to Juneau with Mr. Barr of Northern Canadian Express. It is "Mr. Barr" to you and everyone else in the whole of Alaska and Canada. Although he is a well known pilot, I suspect him of having a terrible first name. We flew down the railroad tracks to Carcross, cut across to Atlin, down the Taku River and over Taku Lodge. I was very anxious to get a glimpse of my home but about that time the plane started jumping up and down. The dogs tried to hang on to the floor with their paws and all wanted to get in my lap. I was having my own troubles trying to stay where I belonged.

We had left Fairbanks 1000 miles north wrapped in winter, and the sun was shining in Juneau and all the snow was gone. We put the dogs in a truck and drove into Juneau. I tied them in back of the Gastineau Hotel where I was stopping. Now my dogs do not howl at night, they are very well mannered, but all the little boys in Juneau came to see them and they had to show their appreciation.

It was not so easy getting the dogs into a plane on floats for the trip back to Taku Lodge. Shell Simmons of the Alaska Air Transport did not have steps for them to walk on. I tried to lift them but he pulled them by the chains around their necks and said "Let's treat these dogs as dogs". I thought he was rather rough with them.

We landed in open water five miles below my lodge. I hitched up the dogs and drove home. It hardly seemed that I'd been gone. The ground was still covered with snow and the river was still frozen.

END.

I did have three months of perfect happiness. I found what I was looking for....I saw into the hearts of men and women and found everything that was good and beautiful there. And if there is a God I have been closer to him than I ever have been before, and if there isn't, then what is my soul longing for?

I know this wilderness is not all desolation. I saw on a dark grey day for one moment God come out and with one sweep of His brush painted the tips of His cottonwood trees to gold.

THIS ORIGINAL MANUSCRIPT IS WITH THE STATE OF ALASKA LIBRARY HISTORICAL COLLECTIONS IN JUNEAU, ALASKA

PART THREE . . . AFTER FAIRBANKS

MARY JOYCE - THE LATE 1930'S

Returning to Taku Lodge in late March, 1936, Mary was enmeshed in her celebrity status though not actively seeking the limelight.

She had time to reflect on how she got here. She had reported for special duty in a Los Angeles hospital in 1926, and the supervisor felt she should warn her about her new patient.. Mary described it thus in an interview: "She said 'Don't be surprised if you are dismissed in the morning. The man has already fired eight others before you.' But I wasn't fired. I stayed with that family for eight years. In 1929 we came to Alaska, into Taku Inlet and up the river in a yacht. To my patient, this hunting lodge, built of logs and perched here on a natural terrace beside the river, surrounded by the beauty of mountains and glaciers, seemed the ideal place to regain his health. He was a Veteran of WWI and was still suffering from the effects of war wounds. He bought the place and it was his home until his death four years later." (They actually moved up the next summer in 1930.)

As the snow was melting, Mary began writing her manuscript and articles, and some short stories about the Taku. The going rate for selling ones writing to a paper or magazine was 5 cents a word.

She started planning a 600-mile dogteam trip from Fairbanks to Nome the next year. She did go to Fairbanks, but got involved in a different project instead. There was mail to answer and daily reports in newspapers to clip that covered her progress on the trail that winter. Her "missing" status, when mercy pilot Joe Crosson was searching for her, was reported in papers from Milwaukee, Los Angeles, Chicago, San Diego, Minneapolis, San Francisco, and Seattle. The Milwaukee Journal sent a telegram to the Army Signal Corps at Tanana Crossing in February 1936 stating:

WILL PAY FOR QUICK EXCLUSIVE
COVERAGE ON SIGNIFICANT DEVEL-
OPMENTS IN SEARCH FOR MARY
JOYCE STOP DISCOVERED DEAD OR
ALIVE STOP WILL ALSO PAY FOR
EXCLUSIVE PICTURES AND HER
STORY IF ALIVE STOP   from State
Editor Milwaukee Journal

She continued opening Taku Lodge summers, welcoming guests. Mary also raised mink, some of whom contributed to her first and only mink coat. There wasn't much she didn't try.

FATHER HUBBARD

Mary was out on the Taku one day in 1937 in her boat when she came across a man stranded on a rock in the middle of the river. His transportation had overturned and he could do nothing.

It happened to be the famous Glacier Priest, Fr. Bernard Hubbard. He and his team of geologists had been studying the glaciers in Alaska for several years A friendship was established and the team made many visits to Taku Lodge.

MARY JOYCE, MOVIE STAR

On March 9, 1937 - the year after her 1,000 mile trip, Mary entered the Mushing Derby in Fairbanks and arrived with Norman Dawn who was working on an upcoming movie in Alaska. Mary decided to become a financial backer, and starred in the film that took place at the lodge and in the surrounding wilderness during 1938.. It also starred a young girl from Juneau, Ann Henning, and two bear cubs who performed some amazing feats. Mary flew in on a float plane and played a character called Taku Mary. I'd looked for the movie for many years on and off... I knew the title was "Orphans of the North" and it was released by Monarch Films.

When I returned from my recent trip to Juneau I got an e-mail from Sean Lanksbury, who was working on the substantial movie correspondence between Dawn and Mary Joyce for the State's Museum Library Archives. He told me "Orphans" was on eBay! I of course purchased it immediately and got to see a younger Mary, although her voice had been dubbed. The photography of the animals (misplaced polar bears, reindeer, penguins...and wolves, brown and black bears, buffalo, birds, fox, caribou, mountain goats and more), the scenery, and the shenanigans of the pair of cubs was outstanding. Norman Dawn himself was the photographer. It was an engaging simple Alaska story with a moral.

Unfortunately, Mary had to fight for years to get some return on her investment. The letters that began "Dear Mary, How was your Christmas and Love, Norman" ended years later with attorneys doing the corresponding. Mary submitted one receipt for 74 cents plus 1 3/5 cents tax,

The male lead was "Popeye" Bob Webster, who played a sourdough in the film named Bedrock Brown, and was keeper of the cubs, Tom and Jerry. In the film he dies on the Mendenhall Glacier. He actually struck gold and died a wealthy man.

The film played in Juneau after continual problems halted the release for a few years. It came out finally in 1940 (and can be googled). 25,000 feet of celluloid film was shot. The "Orphans Report #10" states it played in 30 cities across the U.S. and foreign countries. I don't know how many reports there were in all.

Mary Joyce, Stewardess, with her
Parka and Home Grown Mink Coat.

Movie Ad for "Orphans of the North"
Starring Mary Joyce, circa 1941

Mary at her Quonset Home in Juneau
during the WWII years.

Fr. Hubbard Saved From Rock by Mary Joyce.

Homestead Cabin of Mary Joyce
Up River from Taku Lodge

FLYING HIGH & THE 1940'S

Mary was a stewardess for three years in the early 40's, between Seattle and Billings Montana. This was in the days when attendants had to be nurses as well. She also was a pilot and built a hangar up at the lodge for a float plane. It was never used as such, but the building is still there. Her flying career ended when she had to make an emergency landing on the Gastineau Channel in Juneau. Anonymous wrote a poem about the event:

Mary had a little plane
In which she'd fly and frisk,
Now wasn't that a silly thing
Her little *

WORLD WAR II AND ALASKA

The Japanese were invading the Aleutian Islands and the Alaska Government was advising everyone in the bush to come into the towns for the duration. Mary bought a quonset hut up near the hospital in Juneau, where she worked as a nurse during some of the war years. She also worked as a radio operator in Nome for a short time...apparently learning those dit darrs she talked about in her manuscript.

TAKU LODGE AFTER MARY

Mary still loved the Taku Valley even though she sold the Lodge to the Royal O'Reillys in the mid 40's. She might winter over at the cabin she had homesteaded prior to the war years, located on the Taku River a few miles from Taku Lodge. If she were there, she worked her trap lines. A bear had gotten inside the cabin once, found molasses, and flour, every edible morsel within, and scattered it all over...he must have thought there was treasure under the bed because it and its stuffing were torn to smithereens, coated. with stickiness, goop and white flour honey paste.. The cabin is still being lived in today.

If she was in Juneau, she was a nurse at the hospital... but summers she was still likely to be found at Taku Lodge with the O'Reillys.

Others who were involved with the Lodge were J. Campbell who had a financial interest with the O'Reillys from 1949, chiefly concerned about winter use for his son, who like Hack Smith, loved the hunting and Taku River life; Norman Banfield from 1963; the Gil Bixby's from 1969; the Ron Maas's from 1971; and Michelle and Ken Ward from 1993 to the present.

The Taku Lodge today offers the Ward's Flight and Feast tour from Juneau to the Lodge, an approximate 25 minute floatplane flight over the Taku River and 5 magnificient glaciers with their deep azure crevasses. It lands on the river between the advancing Hole in the Wall glacier and the Taku Lodge where inside they serve up the most delicious salmon bakes during the summers, often complete with visiting bears who come to investigate the outside salmon pit. Ward & Staff stress proper measures to take should you see wildlife.

JOSEPHINE CRUMRINE

In the early 1940's, Mary and her dogs were subjects of Artist Josephine Crumrine. She did 2 pastel portraits of Mary Joyce and her dog Wolf... one is in the Alaska State Museum in Juneau, and Kate Greiner Murray has the other. Crumrine was a well known Alaskan artist whose series of dog portraits done for the covers of the menus of the Alaska Steamship Co. were extremely popular. The 90,000 menus printed were soon depleted.

SUN VALLEY

Mary spent one winter at Sun Valley. She took a team of Siberian Huskies and sled to Central Idaho, and gave moonlight rides. She also drove in the local races. The dogs were in crates for 11 days which I imagine is the reason she didn't go back.

Mary Joyce at the Top Hat Bar in Juneau

1950'S ON ...

    I don't know a lot about what happened with Mary in the 50's and 60's. I do know she appeared on floats and with her dogs in local parades...cut the ribbon to start the Iditerod in 1974 or 75. And people always wanted to talk with her about her 1,000 miles

CANDIDATE FOR TERRITORIAL OFFICE

Mary ran a campaign for territorial representative to the Alaskan Legislature in 1950, but lost. She received a congratulatory letter from then Governor Ernest Gruening, enclosing "a speech giving reasons why people should vote Democrat that might be helpful."

TOP HAT

She bought the Top Hat Bar on South Franklin in Juneau and the Club 22 on Douglas Island, across the bridge from Juneau. A friend of hers, Herb Calloway, ran that for a while.

In the late 60's, Mary was always at the Top Hat on South Franklin, basically only sleeping at her apartment around the corner at the Ferry Way Rooms. It was such a welcoming place because you tended to know almost everyone in town. There was only one movie playing at a time, TV programs came by mail (first to Anchorage, then Fairbanks, then Juneau) three weeks old, and on the first nice Sunday in spring, everyone drove out to the end of the road. So I guess you could say there wasn't a lot to do, especially winters.. Organized tourism hadn't really started yet.

Bars were places to meet your friends, more like a coffeehouse today. A surprising percentage of regulars didn't drink... of course a lot did. And just in case you hadn't had enough to drink by 2:00 or 3:00 a.m. in Juneau, Mary would take a taxi full of friends over the bridge to Douglas and open her Club 22, where the closing hour was 5:00 a.m.

The Top Hat was a favorite spot of the local Irish. I think Mary adopted them all... and a lot of the legislators dropped by.

IRELAND

    She took two trips to Ireland... one with the Grant Brothers, to their home in Donegal, and while in Dublin, delivered a letter from Governor Egan of Alaska to the Lord Mayor of Dublin. And she, my mother and I went over in 1972 to search our family trees. While in Westport, County Mayo, we found a lady married to a Joyce, and discovered an almost-cousin whom I hadn't yet met. Her relative, Bridget Reilly, had just arrived in Alaska and was living temporarily in my cabin back in Juneau.

LUCKY LADY & BEYOND

Later Mary Joyce obtained the Pamaray Club across the street from the TopHat which she remodeled in 1973-4 with the help of her Irish friends, led by Joe Winters. She called it the Lucky Lady...because she said that's what she was... lucky. She lived in the apartment above the bar to the end.

I described her death in 1976 earlier. It was just always so different after that day. She left us all with terrific stories to recall and laugh about.

The McKelveys, Neil Brogan and I took over the Lucky Lady, keeping it in tact for the time being for Mary Joyce. (Brogan still runs it today) The display and map I made for Mary for the Lucky Lady opening is still found on the back wall.

Her Top Hat Bar was run for years by a friend, Marcelo Quinto, until he was forced to move the license out to Mendenhall Valley due to problems with a Top Hat foundation built on pilings.

When I was in Juneau recently (it had been 23 years), I called the cemetery to see if they could tell me where Mary's grave was... I couldn't remember. The man who answered knew right where it was without looking it up, and said he'd have his men who were working in that section put a red flag on it so we'd find it easily. But that's Juneau for you, as I remember it.

I'm truly happy to have been able to share part of Mary Joyce's life with her... and now to share her story with you. It was a very good life indeed!

If you have a Mary Joyce story, I'd love to hear from you....
magreiner@hotmail.com

ABOUT AUTHOR

The author, Mary Anne Greiner, is a relative of Mary Joyce. As a youngster in Wisconsin she remembers visits of her famous cousin from Alaska, attired in stylish suits and hats from the 20's and 30's, always with a touch of doghair from her beloved huskies.

After earning a degree in Journalism from Marquette University, a tour in the Navy, and 2 Peace Corps stints in Iran and Micronesia, Greiner moved to Juneau in 1969. She relished her several years near Joyce, learning much about her 1,000 mile story and joining her twice at the Taku Lodge. She was with Mary Joyce when she died in Juneau in 1976, and promised herself she'd write Mary's story someday...someday is 30 years later.

Greiner's favorite sport is driving the Alcan (Alaska Canada Highway). Three trips so far, and hopefully more to come... experiencing in summer parts of the land Joyce mushed in the winter of 1935-36.